Apple Pies

Apple Pies and Promises:
Motherhood in the Real World

compiled by
Linda Hoffman Kimball

CFI
Springville, Utah

ISBN: 1-55517-849-9
e.1

Published by Cedar Fort, Inc.
www.cedarfort.com

Distributed by:

Typeset by Natalie Roach
Cover design by Nicole Williams
Cover design © 2005 by Lyle Mortimer

Printed in the United States of America
10 9 8 7 6 5 4 3 2 1

Printed on acid-free paper

Dedication ⟋⟋◦

To my mother and my children

Table of Contents

Introduction

I know a name, a glorious name, dearer than any other.
Listen, I'll whisper the name to you; it is the name of mother.
—"The Dearest Names," *Children's Songbook*, 208.

As Latter-day Saint women, our relationship to motherhood is powerful. This is true whether we're remembering our mothers and grandmothers, thinking of our own offspring and the future, or wondering where we fit into the motherhood puzzle.

In our media-driven society, motherhood is often trivialized, undervalued, or sentimentalized. Aren't all nostalgic values supposedly summed up in the cliché "Mom, the flag, and apple pie"? According to much common thought, mothers are either the self-sacrificing women whose cradle-rocking hands rule the world, or they are the root of every neurosis. At church, motherhood is the stuff of praise and power, and sometimes pedestals and puffery.

What is motherhood really?

If you're looking for a tidy answer to that question, you will have to look elsewhere. If you want to share in the real-life, real-world experiences and thoughts of LDS mothers and daughters, read on. In these pages there are glimpses into the complexities and ambivalences of motherhood. Perhaps you will recognize yourself in some of these segments. Maybe you will at last be able to forgive yourself for not living up to an impossible image, realizing you are in good company. Like the intricacies of motherhood itself, these pages may inspire you, mortify you, make you laugh, make you cry, maybe even make you feel "to sing the song of redeeming love" (Alma 5:26).

Eve, "the mother of all living" (Moses 4:26), demonstrated

determination to fulfill her covenants to do God's will. By keeping her promises, she launched her own mortal life and set in motion all of ours. Her choice came at an unimaginable cost. Like us, she shouldered her tasks in the lone and dreary world. Surely her children brought her joy. We know that they also brought her grief. We have no record of how she felt or what she thought. But in the following pages, some of Eve's twenty-first century daughters speak their minds with courage, determination, candor, good humor, and poignancy. Could it be that, so many generations later, these are qualities we inherited from her?

I have enjoyed compiling this collection from many thoughtful, articulate, and real women. You will find no prissiness here—no froth or fastidiousness. The contributors address issues of motherhood from all perspectives. Some write poignantly about elderly mothers, some write hilariously about life with preschoolers, some write about infertility, some write about the struggles of blended families. There are stories of transition, insight, patience, impatience, love, longing, and loss. All of the contributors are LDS women, but not all are mothers themselves. Yet, they are, of course, all daughters.

Relax and read on. Muse. Ponder. Expect the unexpected. If motherhood teaches anything, it teaches that!

Making the decision to have a child is momentous. It is to decide forever to have your heart go walking around outside your body.

—Elizabeth Stone, author and professor

The Reluctant Mother

Lael Littke

"I look like a bellicose buffalo," I said morosely as I gazed into the bedroom mirror at my bloated image.

My husband, George, looked up from the book he was reading. "What does bellicose mean?"

I sighed. "What does anything mean? I've lost my identity. I'm an incubator, not a person." I waddled over to the bed and fell onto it. "I want to cancel delivery."

"Eight and a half months too late for that," George murmured.

I'd get no sympathy from him. He was eager to greet our firstborn. I wasn't. Although I had a wonderful mother, I didn't have a clue how to *be* one. Something had been left out of my ingredients. I had no maternal gene.

But my biological clock was ticktocking. After five years of marriage, I'd figured it was time to get on the mommy track or forget it. So maybe we'd go ahead and order a baby. A small one. A beginner's model. I hoped it would come with an owner's manual.

Things went well for several months. No morning sickness. I continued working, taking the subway each day to my office in midtown Manhattan. I liked working.

Then it all got ridiculous. People cast worried glances my way when I lumbered aboard the subway. Was I going to subdivide right there in the tunnel under the East River? I quit work. I stayed home and worried. Even a baby shower with lots of darling, doll-like clothes didn't activate my motherhood motor.

The big day came. *My last moment of freedom,* I thought mutinously as I was wheeled into the delivery room.

Fast-forward three hours.

"It's a girl," announced Dr. Birnbaum.

I heard a strong wail. My daughter.

A nurse laid her on my right arm. I looked down at her, and she rolled her eyes to look up at me! Suddenly, within a breath, I was a fanged tigress, willing to tear apart anything that might threaten this tiny creature. I knew I could be a hissing snake, a raging grizzly, a berserk eagle, if necessary, to defend my offspring.

"I'll be darned," I whispered. "Is this motherhood?"

It was. Part of it. I soon discovered endless other aspects. Gentleness, tenderness, pure love, joy. It was as if a locked box inside of me had sprung open, spilling out magical jewels I didn't know I possessed.

It's been an adventure—all these years since I had that baby and incredibly became a mother. I chuckle at a wily God who buried all the proper instincts so deep within me that I didn't realize they were there until I was ready to use them. And I thank him.

Prayer on Wheels

Heather Sundahl

Wednesday morning the kids and I pile into Ruby, our '88 Corolla, planning to do our volunteer Meals on Wheels delivery. I'm running late and my heart lurches as I try to start the car. It will barely turn over, and the lights and dash keep going dim every time I turn the key. Jonah keeps saying, "Is it broken? Is it the battery?" His toy-motivated assumption that batteries power the world is correct in this case.

My first instinct is to pray. We need to get these meals to the elderly people on our route. Then there is that moment of fear—what if we pray and the car doesn't start? Will Jonah think prayers don't work? That God doesn't care if the old people eat? So I say a silent pre-prayer that our prayer will be answered for Jonah's sake as well as our hungry charges. So we both pray; I pump the gas, turn the ignition and "Vroom vroom," Ruby starts up.

Jonah is so impressed.

"We prayed and Heavenly Father listened, Mom," he tells me.

I am so happy because I can remember being really little, our cat getting lost, praying with my mom and then finding it. That made a big impression on me. I knew then that God *does* listen and *does* help us out.

So we deliver our meals (I leave Ruby running) and then head to the grocery store because, having been gone on vacation for a week, we are out of everything. I pile the kids and eight bags of groceries into the car and go to start the engine, and it won't. It doesn't even turn over.

Jonah immediately says, "Let's pray, Mom. Then it'll start. Heavenly Father will make it not broken."

Pause. I am panicky again. I do not have faith that mountains can be moved unless those mountains really, really,

really need moving and for some reason the bulldozers don't work. I'm thinking to myself, this is not an emergency anymore. Sure, my ice cream may melt if we don't get moving, but no longer are there hungry old people depending on us for their food. So I try to give Jonah a mini-lecture on not expecting God to do for us what we can manage on our own, but he just keeps insisting we pray.

So I say a prayer that the car will start but add "and if it won't, help us to find a friend to come get us," which seemed to me a reasonable request. The car does *not* start, and so I grab the just-for-such-semi-emergencies cell phone and dial my friend Lisa.

Jonah says, "Hey, Mom, who ya callin'? God?"

It was so cute.

"No, hon. One of his helpers," I reply.

Lisa is not only home but has another friend there so she can rush over *sans* kids and rescue us. And the ice cream, though mushy, was not melted, a little miracle in itself. Jonah seemed a bit confused about why the car wouldn't start after our prayer, but it didn't shake the impact of our earlier success.

Several times this week he has said, "Our car was broken, but it worked because we prayed." Tonight I heard him tell the little boy upstairs that our car was broken and we prayed and God made the battery work because the old people needed Meals on Wheels. I have said several prayers of thanksgiving for this little incident. Faith can be so fragile, and I am so glad that Jonah's little mustard seed seems to be planted in fertile ground.

Folk Wisdom

E. Victoria Grover

When I started my little medical practice in a rural part of northern Maine, one of my first patients was a tiny elderly woman who came in for a physical. Among the routine questions I asked her was how many children she had, and I almost fell out of my chair when she cheerfully answered "fourteen." At the time I had one child of my own who kept me so busy that the thought of multiplying that by fourteen was almost unimaginable.

Seeing my distress, she hastened to reassure me.

"Raising fourteen children in those days was easy. You got 'em all up in the morning, gave 'em mush or eggs for breakfast, and shooed them out the door. Only difference in winter is you got their coats and mitts on first. The older ones took care of the little ones and stayed out of my way, 'cause they knew if I caught 'em I'd put 'em to work! They all learned to entertain themselves."

She sighed and continued.

"Kids today don't get left on their own nearly enough. They don't know how to put four sticks together and build a fort. My granddaughter has more trouble trying to bring up two kids today then I ever had with my fourteen—and her kids are always complainin'. My kids had to work hard sometimes, and they didn't have much toys, but they had more fun than hogs on ice just runnin' around, out by themselves!"

She was right I realized. Sometimes the best thing you can do for your kids is to leave them alone!

A handful of mother wit is worth a bushel of learning.

—Spanish proverb

Feisty Women

Ann Stone

My mother was a quiet, self-effacing woman who never liked to be the center of attention. She seemed most comfortable in the kitchen where she performed with the precision and expertise expected of a daughter of Mormon pioneer stock. She produced bread, rolls, pies, biscuits, and Sunday roasts without cookbooks or recipes. "Handfuls of this, a pinch of that," she would say if asked how anything was made. She deferred to my father in most matters and was cheerful and accepting of her role. Yet, it is through her maternal line that I can trace my roots to some very feisty and spirited women.

Once, when I was flexing my newly discovered "I am woman, hear me roar" muscles, my father said, with some measure of disapproval, "You sound just like Louisa Barnes Pratt." I was pleased. Louisa is my great-great grandmother on my mother's side. She left a journal that was published by the Daughters of the Utah Pioneers, which I had read when I was in college. Louisa was a convert to the Church during the Nauvoo period and suffered great hardships, many precipitated by the long absences of her husband.

Her ability to survive on her own while raising four daughters is one of the qualities that drew me to her. (My husband died when our sons were seven and nine.) Her husband was sent to Tahiti on a mission before the pioneers fled Nauvoo, and she crossed the plains alone with those four girls. She spent very little time with her husband, Addison, after that. She was, for most of her life, what has been termed a Mormon missionary widow.

I remember particularly a quote in her journal that leapt off the page and made me believe I was in the company of an extraordinary woman. It must speak to others as well because it appears on a plaque along the Trail of Hope in Nauvoo. During the first days of the Saints' westward trek, the women saw the need to organize themselves. Louisa writes that she was appointed counselor and scribe and then announces, "Resolved . . . if the men wish to hold control over women let them be on the alert. We believe in equal rights." You go, girl!

There are many more Louisa stories that fuel my inner strong-woman voice, not the least being her savvy engineering of a mission call to join her husband in Tahiti by talking to one of Brigham Young's wives. But that is a story for another time.

My other great-great grandmother, Celia Mounts Hunt (for whom my mother was named), was another dynamic woman. She was one of the few women to accompany the Mormon Battalion on their mission to fight in the Mexican War (her husband, Jefferson Hunt, was a captain in the battalion). But the story that best expresses her unique qualities took place in Nauvoo where the Hunt family had settled along Bear Creek, some twenty-five miles south of the city. They had a small farm that Celia maintained since Jefferson had duties as a member of the Nauvoo Legion and was also working on construction of the Nauvoo Temple after the death of Joseph Smith.

By then the Saints were being harassed by their enemies. Homes and farms in the outlying areas had been burned or ransacked. People were fearful and on edge. Late one afternoon the Hunts were working in the garden digging potatoes when Jefferson saw a group of thugs approaching. He told Celia that he believed they had come for him, "so I'll just hide in the willows close by."

Celia, not to be intimidated, held out a huge, crooked potato, which in the waning light could have easily been mistaken for a pistol, and dared them to come closer. The story goes that she accompanied her "pistol" with a barrage of strong language. Since she was a tough frontierswoman, she had no difficulty finding the words to use. The gang of ruffians departed in due haste. Again: You go, girl!

My mother, Celia, died when I was still in my twenties. There's a good chance that I would have seen beyond her domestic skills to discover those same feisty genes in her. I needed a little more time to grow up. Somehow, it takes a daughter longer to recognize the qualities in her own mother that she sees so clearly in others. Certainly, my mother passed some of those strong-willed tendencies on to me, for better or for worse. I now see glimmers of that same energy in my little granddaughter Elizabeth Ann when she pushes my hand away because she can "do it myself." Long live feisty women!

Mama and the Visitors
Lael Littke

I was eight on that hot summer day when the missionaries came. They were not of our church. I was aware that they had come by in past summers to our Idaho farming community and that my mother had spoken politely to them. She said that if she expected people to be nice to our Mormon missionaries out in the world, it was only right that she be nice to those from other churches.

Some people in town weren't. One of my good friends told me we should hide when they came. She said they would take over our minds and twist them around to follow someone other than our good bishop. She said we kids should be especially careful because they might grab us and steal us away. She said we should throw rocks at them and drive them off.

So when the battered old green car turned into our driveway, I slunk behind the house to pick up a stone. Mama, who was working in a flower bed, rose to greet the two men and two women who got out of the car. They looked tired and dusty. "Come over here in the shade," she said. "Would you like lemonade? I just made some."

"Bless you, Sister," said one of the men. "That would be wonderful."

I watched the four suspiciously as my mother went into the house. I was ready to run in case they made a move to grab me and steal me away.

They sat down under our weeping willow tree. One of the women stretched out flat on the cool grass. When Mama brought the lemonade in tall glasses clinking with ice, they thanked her and began to talk. Mama nodded frequently and responded as if she believed all they were saying. Were they twisting her mind? Would they grab *her* and steal her away?

I gripped the rock in my hand.

Before they left, Mama took them to our garden where she helped them pick corn and dig potatoes. She pulled up bunches of radishes and carrots for them. I was astounded when she went back to the house and brought out a loaf of her freshly baked bread, plus a huge hunk of the roast beef we'd had for our midday farm dinner. For sure they had taken over her mind! There wouldn't be enough left for us to eat with our bread-and-milk supper!

Before they drove away, they gave her a book, which she accepted graciously. Still clutching my rock, I watched them go. Then I turned to my mother.

I wondered if I dared scold her for welcoming those strangers, for talking to them, for endangering me! I boiled it all down to one question.

"Mama!" I said sternly. "Why did you feed them?"

She boiled it all down to one answer, which has resonated down through the years.

"Because they were hungry," she said.

Long-term Parenting

Connie Susa

"What is your philosophy of motherhood?"

My mother asked me this question in a rare, quiet moment while my sisters and their families were gathered with us at a holiday dinner. I observed a significant pause in forks and gravy boats around me as they waited for my answer.

"I believe my role is to work my way out of the job," I braved.

The stillness deepened as each person waited for further explanation.

Given that clear mandate, I continued describing how I wanted to help our three boys gain the knowledge and skills necessary to live independent and contributory lives. I recalled the guideline given by a BYU professor that each time we added a privilege to our maturing children, we needed to add a responsibility as well. I gave examples of how I planned to fade control as our boys increased in wisdom, stature, and favor.

When I finished my discourse, my mother raised her napkin slowly to her lips, dabbed them quite deliberately, wiped back across her mouth, raised her well-tweezed eyebrows and finally announced, "Well, I suppose you are entitled to your opinion." Shamed by her obvious disapproval, I focused on my plate, and ordinary conversation mercifully resumed.

As life erected various obstacles to launching our three, now-grown, sons, I have often thought back to my certain answer and felt it morphing within me. Joe and Frank, now in their early thirties, have marked significant milestones in their adult journeys. Our youngest son, Mark, at twenty-seven, however, is still here at home with us, dependent in several ways.

Mark uses a wheelchair and hearing aids, and he has the support of two other mothers, paid to help with his work and physical training. In addition, we have assembled a network of friends, a Personal Lifetime Advocacy Network, who have committed to help him problem-solve and maintain his membership in the community beyond the deaths of my husband and me. Each is involved in his life now, to solidify the relationship and to practice their roles so that he can continue as normally as possible after we pass beyond the veil.

Even so, I often contemplate the statue of the mother, *Preparing Her Son*, in the Relief Society Garden in Nauvoo. Like her, I stand behind my son, hands-on and fixed permanently in the role of preparation. Another aging mother of an adult with disabilities, weighing alternatives that would further constrain her son in the future, once told me that for her "death is not an option."

For me, death is not only an option, but as I approach my seventh decade, it is a looming certainty. Like my husband, I have cherished raising our three boys under the covenant that made us an eternal family. I no longer determine to work myself out of this job of mothering. I see the possibility of eternal increase as something that I have literally been preparing for all of my adult life. Perhaps the statue of the Nauvoo mother is standing behind her son because he is leading her into her future.

By Proxy

Linda Hoffman Kimball

I signed up to go with my son, Chase, to the upcoming youth baptismal trip. I also got my gumption up to be baptized for my mother, dead nine years now. She hadn't been pleased with my joining the Church back when I was in college. Time and friendliness softened most of her disgruntlement, but in my mind she remained vaguely annoyed and embarrassed by my being Mormon.

My son and husband were in the kitchen when I made the call, getting final instructions about when to show up at the temple and what to bring. When I hung up, I shuddered and said to Chris and Chase, "She's gonna kill me. My mom is gonna kill me."

It was a busy weekend. Not only did we have the baptismal trip on Saturday, but I also had to prepare Sunday's Relief Society lesson, "Comfort in the Hour of Grief." Chase and I went to the baptistery and waited for our turns. I kept praying for my mom not to be upset about this. I didn't feel any particular presence either way—no chill shiver of beyond-the-veil umbrage, and no warm glow of approval. I plowed on, got baptized on her behalf, and puddled prayerfully and reverently back into my regular clothing.

Back at home, I threw myself into preparation for the Relief Society lesson. There was obvious irony to the lesson topic. My mother's death still seemed fresh in many ways. And, after a day filled with the temple and its enormous implications for "comfort in the hour of grief," my mind was swirling with thoughts of my mom and the eternities in general.

I decided that talking about my mother, her passing, and some of the comfort I found at the time of my mother's death was appropriate to integrate into the lesson. Being a firm believer in the power of good visual aids, I decided to locate some of my mom's smaller quilts and handwork to give a sense of who my mom was.

I found a few of the gems she made for my kids when they were little and spied a bulging pillowcase up high in my closet. I couldn't remember what was in it. I poked it down off the shelf and recognized the yellowed lace scraps that fell out as the leftover material from my mother's wedding dress.

This apparently was one of my mom's many fabric bundles I'd inherited when my sisters and I cleaned out her place at her death. I had never seen the wedding dress. My sisters had. No one knew where it was now. I thought that maybe some scraps of fabric from her dress might make good additions to the visual aids for my lesson.

I began to pull the contents carefully from the yellowing pillowcase. There were lots of odd-shaped swatches of lovely, aged lace. Then something in paper emerged—it was the pattern she had used to make the dress! And something else came out—a small bag of tiny buttons that, according to the pattern, were what she had used on her dress. I reached in further. Now I found something netted, with brittle, waxy nobs—my mother's wedding veil! I pulled that out, put it on my head, and began to feel my eyes fill. There was still something left in the pillowcase. I pulled out the last wadded yardage wrapped haphazardly in tissue paper. I carefully shook out the lump of lace and satin. This was it! My mother's wedding dress!

Even though I wasn't as svelte as my mother was at her wedding, I tried it on. As long as I didn't zip it up at the side, the dress fit. I stared at myself in the mirror, wearing my mother's dress and veil, on the very day that I had been baptized on her behalf. Tears flowed freely now. I felt as though by slipping my arms into sleeves she wore on her most significant day, she was putting her arms around me, embracing me by proxy.

Whatever her feelings are about my doing temple work for her, I feel assured that, no, she is not going to kill me. She is a living being still, moving beyond annoyance and embarrassment and at least into gratitude for my offering to her. I love you, Mom.

The Dress

Kelly Austin

It came to me in such a circuitous, yet inspired way—that dress. A ward member, neighbor, and friend of my mother's gave her a bundle of little dresses. Handmade in Portugal, the antique dresses had been searched out by the woman's mother and sister when she learned of her pregnancy, hoping finally for a daughter.

I can see those Portuguese women embroidering the delicate fabric, adding smocking, edging, flowers, scalloped hems, and buttons smaller than my smallest fingernail. A labor of love for new life.

She gave the dresses to my mother when her pregnancy—a daughter at last—ended in stillbirth. There would be no others. My mother's friend would have to give up her dream of raising a daughter, in this life at least.

My mother was pregnant with me, her first daughter. I wore those dresses. So did my sister. And so did our dolls. They were well loved, those dresses, one ripped at the neck when little hands could not (or would not) unfasten the tiny buttons.

I have two sons. When I became pregnant for the third time, we all prayed for a daughter. My youngest son, then four, had told me before I even knew we were going to have another child that he needed a sister, that he knew there was a sister who just hadn't been born yet. I sensed this daughter but dared not fix my hopes too tightly—after all, until this generation, my husband's family hadn't produced a daughter in nearly a hundred years. Or so the legend goes.

We learned this baby was indeed a girl at the same time we learned she had a genetic disorder that would mean she would have, at most, a few months of life. Weeks later, we were told to hope for hours at best. We went from planning her birth to planning her funeral.

I had planned on having her blessed in the same dress I was blessed in. But to bury her in my blessing dress also meant burying hopes of a daughter to raise. Besides, maybe my sister—who had also been blessed in the same dress—would be more fortunate.

I asked my mother about those dresses. Curiously, she had recently found them, laundered them, and restored them to a more pristine condition than two schoolgirls had left them. She sent them to me.

They were all the purest white, except one. It bore the slightest hint of pink so faint that it had to be next to another dress to tell. A blush, a rose in bloom. Color waiting to happen. Much as I avoided pink before, I chose this dress. The color seemed appropriate, indicative of her vibrant spirit, of the joy she brought into our lives. Of the not-quite-fulfilled dreams of raising a daughter.

We had hoped for a few hours with our daughter. But time was not to be ours. Ani died three weeks before my scheduled induction. I awoke one morning to stillness, her death confirmed later that afternoon by an all-too-still and silent ultrasound. I could no longer pretend she might wake up.

We buried her in that pale dress—far too big for her small body, but beautiful in its significance. That dress went from devoted hands crafting its beauty to a loving mother and sister bestowing a gift, hoping for their daughter and sister to have a baby girl of her own. It rested for a brief time with her, a bereaved mother letting go of hope. Then it went to a joyful mother, welcoming her first daughter. That infant daughter filled the dress with long-awaited life. The dress came full circle again to another bereaved mother, that little girl, letting go of her own daughter. The dress completed a powerful circle of women celebrating life and motherhood in all its varied and sometimes fleeting forms.

Now, the rest of those dresses, as well as my blessing dress, await another daughter, Ani's unborn sister. The circle continues. I'm sure Ani approves.

The Circle

Sue Gong

Roused by a faint cry from upstairs at the far corner of the house, I was up and halfway there before I was fully awake. I knew who it was. Two-year-old Brinley was homesick for her mom, who was in the hospital with Brinley's newborn brother. The child had sobbed herself out in my arms and then had chosen to sleep near my daughters, thirteen-year-old Gloria Jean and eleven-year-old Angela.

Arriving at Brinley's bedside, I found her asleep again. Angela was there.

"A hurt from inside woke me up when she cried," Angela whispered. "I patted her back for a minute, and she went right to sleep."

Gloria Jean appeared beside us. There we stood in a small circle, the three of us, light in our various nightdress, surrounded by the dark in the silent house, the boys nearby undisturbed.

A deep, ancient current of understanding and tenderness connected us in our wakefulness. I knew then that I had become the mother of women.

Pondering Pitchers

Kathryn Loosli Pritchett

Until I saw them lined up on the dining room table waiting to be stored, I hadn't realized how many pitchers I owned. First there were my fancy pitchers: the red cut glass pitcher that casts ruby shadows on the tablecloth, the clear glass pitcher for Sunday dinner, the battered "hotel silver" pitcher I won as a door prize, the green pedestal pitcher perfect for lemonade on the deck, the antique basalt-wear pitcher I gave my husband for his forty-fourth birthday, and the little Art Deco pitcher we picked up in Paris last summer at Hemingway's favorite brasserie.

Then there were the more utilitarian pitchers: the blue ceramic pitcher that matched my old kitchen and still cheers me with its portly dimensions, the small square glass pitcher that fits so nicely in the refrigerator door, the speckled stoneware pitcher that my in-laws brought me from a trip back east, and the groovy orange plastic pitcher that I bought long distance from my sister so she could qualify for the Tupperware party hostess gift.

How had all these pitchers made their way to my home? I wasn't consciously collecting them, but nevertheless there they were. And I wasn't willing to part with one of them. I had been taught at my mother's table that pitchers are an essential element of a proper home.

My siblings' spouses will tell you that one of the first Loosli family rules they learned was that my mother didn't allow jugs, cartons, or bottles on her table. Even if it meant one more dirty dish in a sink filled to overflowing with the dinnerware necessary to feed a family of eleven, the proper way to serve a beverage was in a pitcher.

My mother married my father when she was nineteen and moved from a small town in Utah to an even smaller farming community in southeastern Idaho. Though she was not one to "put on airs," she was nevertheless determined that we would be raised with good manners. One of the outward displays of her child-rearing philosophy was a properly set table, including a tablecloth at every meal, full place settings, and a pitcher on the table.

My brothers might be sitting at the table in mud-encrusted work clothes from their early morning chores, a newborn calf rescued from the midnight cold might be lowing in the basement, and the dust from the potato fields might be obscuring the view of the Tetons outside our window, but the milk would be served in a pitcher.

When I was newly married with a table of my own to set, I tended to ignore the teachings of my youth. A gallon of milk would provide the centerpiece at the breakfast table, a carton of orange juice at its side. After work, I'd quickly prepare dinner, and we'd sit down with those same jugs and cartons or maybe a can of soda close at hand. Once our children came along, the mealtime chaos precluded anything more formal than a "tippy cup" as a beverage container.

But now that my kids are older and no one's flinging peas across my table or using their shirtfronts as napkins, pitchers make regular appearances at our meals. Could it be that I'm finally following my mother's example because I'm feeling threatened by the wilderness outside my own doors?

Though I'm not raising my family in the wilds of Idaho, I still battle the clear and present dangers of drugs, sex, and—oh, give me the innocence of rock and roll—explicit song lyrics. Even the time demands of my children's "wholesome" activities—sports practices, music lessons, study groups—continually encroach upon my civilized family life.

Placing a pitcher on the table may be a small defense

against the rush of modern life. And yet, having watched my mother wield a pitcher successfully, I'm hoping that I can also keep the wilderness at bay through proper dinnerware.

What Mom Left Us

Linda Hoffman Kimball

Mom was an avid quilter who lived and died by the adage, "She who dies with the most fabric, wins." She won—no doubt about it.

About a month after my mother's death at seventy-eight, I had a dream. In my dream—as it really had been during the three weeks she lay comatose in the hospital—my two grieving sisters and I scurried around her apartment trying to locate her important papers, clean out her appliances, drawers, and closets, and sort her belongings—her mountains of crafts and fabric. Unlike our real experience, in my dream every time one of us opened any kind of door, out would tumble a quilt. Quilts in the kitchen cupboards. Patchwork wonders in the china cabinet. Batted beauties in the bathroom. They were each colorful, luxuriant, abundant, welcoming, and everywhere! In my dream, I was confused about what was happening. Then I suddenly understood!

"Look!" I announced to my sisters in the dream. "We don't have to be so sad! She knows we're grieving, but Mom has left us all these *comforters*!"

Now, ten years after her death, I take great *comfort* in this memory, especially when I snuggle up with one of her beautiful handmade quilts.

Competitive Mothering

Heather Sundahl

One of my least proud mothering moments happened just weeks after Jonah's birth (I wasted no time in screwing up). Now, I do not think of myself as a competitive person in general. As the youngest child in an overachieving family, anything I did had already been done earlier and better by at least one of my siblings. So most of the time I thought, "Why try to be the best?" This encouraged my type-B personality, and as a result I stayed away from things competitive in nature. But there are times when someone has challenged me in such a way that I pull out all the stops and become a competitive lunatic.

So here's how it happened this time. There was a woman in our birthing class who always played topper. If I said I'd gone on an eating binge and snarfed two Big Macs, she'd reply that she'd had three *and* a Filet-o-Fish. No matter what I said, she'd had it worse, seen it more, experienced it more acutely.

After our kids were born (she also had a boy), things just got worse. She told me that she and her husband had also considered naming their son Jonah but then decided against it "because we don't want him being mocked because of his name." I was sooo bugged! It's not like we named our kid Scooby Doo. I prided myself in resisting the urge to play topper back. I'd just smile and try to not let my irritation show. But she kept commenting on how much bigger her baby was than Jonah. No big deal—size schmize. I should have let it go, but she kept making me feel like my kid was wasting away in comparison with her hearty hunk in Huggies when, in fact, Jonah and this kid were roughly the same size. So one day on the phone she said to me, "I can't believe how much bigger my Bobby is than Jonah, and Jonah is two weeks older too."

So I did a bad thing. I baited her and I asked her a question to which I already knew the answer. "So tell me how much he weighed at his one-month appointment." (She'd told me six times already.)

"Oh, Bobby's a whopping nine pounds fourteen ounces."

"Golly," I said all sweetly. "Jonah was ten pounds ten ounces at his."

I thought that would put a cork in her bragging mouth.

But she didn't miss a beat and retorted, "Bobby can roll over."

It was a total non sequitur, but I was stunned and stumped. She had declared an all-out baby topper war, and I was not about to lose—especially since I clearly had the superior offspring.

One-month-olds do not, as a rule, roll over, and Jonah had not so much as leaned in one direction or the other. I had some serious work to do. I quickly got off the phone and called Dave at work. "Dave, you need to come home early. We have to teach this baby to roll over."

I must add that although Dave was thoroughly disgusted with me, he is still the supportive husband and did in fact come home and help me teach Jonah to roll over. Jonah adored his mobile, this one dangling monkey in particular. So we put him on his belly, turned on the mobile, and placed the monkey in his side vision and then slowly moved the monkey above him. He tried to follow it, lifted and turned his giant cranium, and the sheer weight of his huge noggin made his body follow. Whoosh, he rolled over at six weeks. I felt proud, but I also felt petty and immature and decided not to engage in baby topper warfare ever again.

It's funny how things are different with second kids. Georgia's six-week mark came and went and, though it occurred to me one day that she was most likely capable of rolling over, I did nothing to encourage it. Just the opposite. Now I knew how dangerous mobility was in any form. I was content when her three-month mark came and still no rolling over. But the other night she was on Jonah's futon and started to roll herself from her back to her belly. Dave and I stepped back, wanting it to be *her* very own accomplishment. As she was halfway there, Jonah reached for her. "Let her do it," I said, thinking he would give her a little push to help her get from her side to her belly. But no, big brother pulled her back to her back. But little Georgia was determined and somehow managed to make it to her stomach. We all cheered. I was the proudest mama in the world.

Tenure

Patricia Shelley Bushman

I was pretty naive about motherhood. As a single woman in my thirties, I still hoped to become a mother. I knew there was time biologically to have a child, but I worried if I had the stamina to raise teenagers if I was in my sixties. I was comforted by the fact that my tenure would only last about eighteen years. When the children graduated from high school and went off to college, my stewardship would come to an end.

This was a silly notion because my own experience as a child proved otherwise. My parents did not cut the apron strings when I went off to college. As I spent time on my own, I became more independent and confident in my ability to take care of myself. However, my parents were always there for me with love and support. Phone calls from them were a weekly ritual. I knew if I ever had concerns I could pick up the phone anytime and I would find compassion and comfort.

The reality of motherhood became more apparent soon after I married. One of my brothers experienced a painful break-up of his marriage, with four children still to raise. When his wife left the family, my mother was on the next plane to their home. She lived with my brother so she could help take care of his four children. Periodically, my father would fly across country to visit her, or my mother would go home for a weekend rest. In her late sixties, she certainly needed it. However, my mother never complained, even though she had no idea how long this mothering job would last.

Two years later my brother fell in love with a wonderful woman who had two children of her own, and they married in the temple. I was lucky because now I needed my mother

31

to take care of me. I was expecting a baby two weeks after my brother's wedding. My mother came to town after my C-section and stayed with us for three weeks. My mom never had a break, but it didn't seem to phase her. She always radiated happiness when serving her family.

I marvel at the inner strength of my mother. She has continually done so much for each of her children, but seeing what she did for my brother in his hour of need was a great example to me. I know her physical presence and emotional support were critical in helping her son and her grandchidren through a difficult time.

My naiveté has been washed away. I now understand that being a mother is a test of endurance. It is a stewardship that will never end. I often feel overwhelmed by the responsibility, but I know if I walk in my mother's footsteps I will do just fine.

The Year of Mothering Intensely

Laurel Madsen

Mothering children takes a lot of intelligence, empathy, love, and stamina—and it doesn't stop when they grow up. If you've got grown-up kids, you already know that, and if you have a passel of little ones, trust me—your challenges will only grow as they grow.

Take this past year; I call it *my year of mothering intensely.* All four of my kids—two married and two in college—needed my listening ear and unconditional love as they dealt with hard challenges. Parents stand ready to help when their children need them—I'm not unique—but all of them at once?

The year began when our oldest daughter, pregnant with her fourth child, brought her small children and came to stay with us while her husband went off to months of Army Ranger training and then to the first Persian Gulf war.

To say it was a difficult time for Marion is a vast understatement. For months before the war began, the media was full of the horrific possibilities the enemy had in store for our troops. Her little boy came home from kindergarten one awful day to ask if it was true, as his classmates said, that his daddy would be killed in the war. Our daughter needed our love and support as never before, especially in helping her keep the children's turned-upside-down world secure and happy.

It had been a long time since we had had young children in our household. Once again, warm little bodies often joined us in our bed in the middle of the night. We changed diapers, applied copious Band-Aids, told stories, made lots of cookies, welcomed the neighborhood children who came to play, and at church on Sunday, snuggled children on our laps as little arms twined around our necks. It was a bittersweet time—the children were a joy, but always on our minds was the knowledge that their father was in harm's way, and their mother was coping with daily fear that he might not return.

But as we sought to give emotional support to Marion and her little ones, our other children needed us too! At BYU, our younger married daughter, Lisa, and her husband were stretched almost beyond their limits as they strove to get him through school. Lisa had managed a full-time job and caring for her two-year-old with equilibrium until she had to cope with a second pregnancy that brought nine months of unrelenting nausea and severe headaches. Our single daughter, Stephanie, a BYU student, had endured the bitter breaking off of an engagement a couple of years before and now had met someone else. She loved him, but she could not bring herself to make a commitment. Our son, Chris, a freshman at a university near our home, had drawn away from the Church during his high school years. Now he was active again at the institute but was torn over whether to go on a mission.

When our children had first gone five hundred miles away to college, we kept the phone lines hot, and many of these calls became known in our family as "call and bawl" talks. Once more, "call and bawl" became common at our house, although now there was nothing laughable or trivial about the tears shed on each side as I listened to our daughters' very real pain—Lisa doubtful she could physically make it through another day; Stephanie not sure she could trust again to try another engagement.

Our son came home each weekend. Chris and I had always been close, and now we often sat up through the night as he agonized over his mission decision. He was drifting back to old ways and friends as he waited, and for me, it was like watching a battle for his soul. The fight went on and on. He put in his papers, received his call, and the date was set for his sacrament meeting farewell. At the last minute Chris felt he was not yet ready and notified the bishop that the farewell should not take place. His decision appeared to be made.

We had all been praying for the Lord's help, and of course he was watching over all of us and hearing our pleading. Even when we did not fully realize it, his hand was in our lives.

Spring came at last after the troubled winter, and I traveled to Utah to welcome my new grandchild there. Lisa was relieved of illness and was full of joy to have a perfect, beautiful daughter. When I returned to Colorado, I was present in the delivery room when Marion's healthy little son came yelling lustily into the world. Three weeks to the day after his birth, his father returned safely from the Persian Gulf, and Marion once again was able to smile. In the meantime, the Spirit touched Chris's heart, and he finally made a firm choice to go on a mission. His last-minute farewell was held in the Relief Society room on a Sunday evening with the whole family there, including Stephanie's new fiancé.

On Mother's Day I counted my blessings—my son-in-law's safe return from war, two new grandbabies, a son happy in the mission field, and my youngest daughter's joy as she planned her temple wedding. That Sunday, several women were especially honored as "special Mormon mothers." I was not one of them, and after the year of mothering intensely, I felt a momentary pang, but then I realized that no one else could know of the challenges our family had met and overcome—of the pain, fear, and despair that my children had come through, with the Lord's help, to find happiness. It was a hard year, and it was a beautiful one, for I was allowed to enter into my children's hearts and to share both their sorrows and their joys.

Woman in the home has not yet lost her dignity, in spite of Mother's Day, with its offensive implication that our love needs an annual nudging, like our enthusiasm for the battle of Bunker Hill.

—John Erskine, author and educator

Thoughts about Mother's Day

Claudia Bushman

I think Mother's Day has come a long way, and all for the better. In my childhood the officials were already dealing with the problems of women who were not mothers, asking all women to stand and handing out carnations to all, red for those whose mothers were alive, white to those whose mothers had moved on. Those carnations were very ratty by the end of church. Since then I have received corsages, awards for having the most children, begonia plants, tomato plants, sentimental little books, and recently nothing to take home but announcements that a donation had been made to a women's shelter. Surely that's a worthwhile progression.

But even then, far back in years, the leaders had found the key to success: focus on the mothers of the mothers. Everyone has a mother. So whenever asked to give a Mother's Day talk, I always talk about my mother and grandmothers, not as perfect people, but as lively, imaginative, interesting, driven women. I focus on the matriarchal line because I think that connection needs more attention in our culture, though I could say good things about my in-laws and my father's lines as well. But face it, we are more the products of our mothers than of our fathers.

For forty years I have felt myself turning into my mother. My father referred to our three-generation line as "The Formidable Gordon Women," and it's a badge we wear with pride. There may actually be something to this Mother's Day business after all.

Having downplayed Mother's Day with my children for years, I am always surprised, touched, and appreciative when they call me on Mother's Day. I love to hear from them. I seldom got breakfast in bed or one of those other traditional loving-hands appreciations, but they have been the most satisfactory and beloved of children. I am grateful for them, their wonderful families, their good lives, and their affection for each other.

If I could have a Mother's Day wish, it would be that our leaders would be more appreciative of the problems of our young mothers. No group gets shorter shrift. We know how hard it is to get several children, or a single baby, ready for church, get them there, and then spend three hours in and out of meetings.

Why aren't our corridors wider to accommodate the strollers, the vehicles of choice where I live? Why are mothers not asked to review the plans for new churches? Why are there not more and better equipped bathrooms? Why have some wards done away with cry rooms? Why don't we shave off an hour from those long blocks? Why do so many fathers sit on the stand? These remain the mysteries of the Church. What is truly impressive is how well mothers do despite their difficulties. Hats off to them on Mother's Day and every day.

A Mother's Day Sunbeam

Ardith Walker

Ever since I was a teenager, my favorite part of Mother's Day was the Primary children singing in sacrament meeting. Just before my husband and I got married, I watched the children with particular interest, trying to pick out the child that looked closest to what I knew our own child would look like. In a few short years, we would be the proud parents watching our own little Sunbeam.

After we were married, a miscarriage followed by infertility threw us all off schedule for my plans of having our own child sing on Mother's Day. I cried every month, but I especially cried on Mother's Day. In this sorry state of mind, I suffered through six Mother's Days without even being pregnant. When I finally did become pregnant, the baby was born three days *after* Mother's Day. A few years later our own little son was at last eligible to sing in sacrament meeting as a fresh, new Sunbeam.

The Primary children marched to the front of the chapel. Scott was front and center where he could be seen and appreciated by all the members of the ward. His fine blond hair shimmered like a halo as the light shone in from the side window, and his bright little face beamed. He was angelic. He was adorable. He was perfect. I could feel the members nearby look at Scott and glance over at me, understanding why I was so delighted. My heart swelled with pride.

As the song started, my beautiful little son's hand wandered down inside the front of his cute little Sunday pants, right to the crotch. I leaned up on the bench, frantically trying to get his attention. I started waving to him, hoping he would wave back. Instead of waving, he stuck his other hand inside his pants. I looked over at my husband; he was waving at Scott with both hands.

Scott smiled as only a Sunbeam could and proudly sang with all his heart.

The Primary sang three songs that day. Scott never did wave. I finally leaned back in my seat, realizing that perhaps Mother's Day might not be all it is cracked up to be.

Motherhood and Halloween

Heather Sundahl

I know that many Mormon mothers have an aversion to store-bought costumes (let's not even get into the mask debate here). There is something that goes against one's pioneer heritage in schlepping to Toys "R" Us and simply buying a Cinderella or pirate or whatever costume. So many of us feel it is more—dare I say "industrious?"—to buy fabric and have needle and thread or hot glue gun at the ready to hand-make our little pumpkin suits or ladybugs.

When I was a kid, my mom would *never* buy a costume (nor would she buy Skippy peanut butter, no matter how much we begged; instead she bought the bishops' storehouse tin can kind that had three cups of oil on the top and ripped the bread when you tried to spread it—as if my very salvation depended on my not having that extra spoonful of sugar in the Skippy that made it so delicious). But she didn't make our costumes either. So we always had to find stuff that we could turn into a costume, like a black leotard would make you a cat, or a swinging skirt and cashmere sweater for a fifties girl (this was when "Happy Days" was all the rage). But I secretly *longed* for a store-bought costume. I lusted over Jill Yamin in her ready-made tooth fairy getup complete with a sparkly wand. I envied Janie Nordblad her saloon girl outfit so much that I borrowed it the following year and loved every second in those smart and sassy duds.

Some will claim it is cheaper, and hence, more industrious to make a costume. A friend of mine recoiled at the Disney store price for a Sleeping Beauty costume, so she set out to make one of her own. In the end, not counting her time or sanity, she spent ten dollars *more* on the homemade version than if she'd bought the one from the store. But there is something special in a one-of-a-kind, homemade costume that makes you feel proud (even if the kid couldn't care less). And many women *love* to sew and find great satisfaction in these creative endeavors.

I can't sew at all. I know many of you say the same thing, but secretly you *did* have a home economics class in seventh grade and have made aprons or *tres facile* dresses. I've heard many a woman swear she can't sew, and then I find out she not only has a machine but knows how to do zippers and linings and buttons—oh my! But when I say I can't sew, I mean it.

Even so, I still feel compelled to *make* a costume for my son Jonah. Last year he was a lion, and I spent twenty hours and three yards of felt trying to get his hat/mane right. Then on Halloween I went to put it on him, and he cried and ripped it off his head. I said, in all seriousness, "You will wear this or I will *bite* you." He cried even harder, and I finally had the sense to bribe him with Smarties to wear it. Am I evil or what?

This year when I asked him what he wanted to be, I hoped he'd say something that I could buy off the rack. Homemade schmomade—I'm pregnant and working and I can't sew. "Please, say 'Winnie the Pooh,'" I was thinking. But no, he tells me he wants to be a bird. Maybe he wants to be Big Bird, I think; maybe there's a Sesame Street store.

Jonah announces in the next breath he wants to be a blue jay. A blue jay, for heaven's sake! My husband, Dave, is an avid birder and has been training Jonah since birth to be the same. By age two Jonah could identify mourning doves while I still thought I'd heard an owl. So I drag out the many bird encyclopedias we have and look up blue jay and draw a simple sketch. Enter Dave, master birder. "Um, Heather, that's nice and all, but the head is shaped more at an angle, and the beak needs to be pointier and shorter. And be sure to remember that a blue jay's feathers are iridescent, so the fabric will need to shimmer."

The next thing you know I am in the Jo-Ann fabric store in the *bridal* section looking at chiffons and taffetas for a two-and-a-half-year-old's Halloween costume that he will wear once (that is, unless he refuses to wear it). Once the fabric is cut, it is too late to turn back, and so now I am trying to figure out how on earth to do this thing. So far I have some blue felt pinned together for the head, with a toilet paper roll cut to resemble a beak, but it just looks like a toilet paper roll with black felt on it. I am too scared to attempt the wings at this point. I will most likely wait until the twenty-ninth and do it in a rush when there is no time to worry if it looks good enough, and no time to do it again if it doesn't. So if any of you out there were thinking of making a costume, think long and hard and then run to Toys "R" Us while they still have your kid's size. A sewing-free Halloween sounds like quite a treat to me.

The Hunt

Lisa Ray Turner

I was a negligent mother. My sons were three and five and I'd never taken them to an Easter egg hunt. I vowed to remedy this oversight by promising to take them to the community Easter egg hunt that year.

I didn't make this promise grudgingly. I wanted to go. Warm, fuzzy images of egg hunts from my childhood filled my mind. I remembered little girls dressed in yellow ruffles and yards of lace, their hair festooned with shiny pastel ribbons. Small boys looked like they'd just come from Sunday School, in their white shorts, starched bow ties, and slicked-back hair.

These images tugged at my heart. I couldn't wait to see my own pink-cheeked boys frolicking in the grass with pastel wicker baskets, laughing as they spied colorful eggs. Oozing with sentimentality, we headed for the city park.

Boy, was I in for a shock. Hoards of children were massed around the park perimeter, waiting for the hunt to begin. They looked like racehorses at the starting gate, wild-eyed and feral. The younger children shoved and pushed, bulldozing their way to the front of the pack. The bigger kids sneered, disdainful of the preschoolers' attempts to find a place in the crowd.

I definitely would not see frolicking today. Sprinting maybe. Possibly front-line combat. But frolicking? Definitely not.

Another thing I wouldn't see was a bow tie or anything remotely resembling a ruffled, yellow dress. The children—boys and girls alike—sported torn blue jeans, stinky Batman T-shirts, and sweat suits that looked like they'd seen too many soccer games.

But it wasn't only the clothes that had changed in thirty

years. So had the baskets. Plastic ice cream tubs and rusty coffee cans replaced the graceful, straw baskets of my childhood. The more optimistic kids carried large, brown grocery sacks or backpacks. Oh, well.

A shrill whistle signaled the start of the hunt, and mobs of blue-jeaned kids ran like bloodhounds onto the field. As my three-year-old inhaled the dust stirred up by the stampeding children, he burst into tears. "All the eggs will be gone," he wailed.

I didn't know what to do. The park pulsed with small bodies. I felt like a bee in a gigantic hive. The man next to me noticed my weeping three-year-old and whispered, "It's crazy, huh? That's why I always bring eggs for my kids to find." Maybe he was onto something. I'd remember his tip for next year.

But I still had this year to get through. We'd come to an Easter egg hunt and, gosh darn it, my kids were going to find eggs. I became a bloodhound myself. Gripping my sons' hands, I said in my best Dirty Harry voice, "Let's go get us some eggs, boys."

We scoured the fields for brightly colored plastic eggs tucked under bushes and hidden in tree branches (real eggs were passé due to concerns about salmonella). After being rammed and maimed by neighboring bloodhounds, my boys finally found some eggs. Their faces glowed as they studied their treasures. Relieved, I proclaimed the hunt a success, and we started for home.

Then we saw two forlorn little girls, their baskets empty, still searching for eggs. "The eggs are gone," their tired-looking mother said. "Let's just go home."

My heart ached for the sad-faced little girls. I looked in my boys' full baskets and knew what we had to do. I suggested to my sons that they give some eggs to the empty-handed hunters.

Even as I asked, I wondered whether I was expecting too much. My sons hadn't had an easy day at the hunt either. Would they give up their hard-won prizes?

To my delight, my boys didn't hesitate before they each sacrificed several candy-filled eggs. The little girls chorused surprised thank-you's and their eyes brightened. Their mother gushed about how sweet my sons were. I joined the gushing and told my sons I was proud of them. We left the park happy, baskets full of tooth-rotting candy, hearts full of goodwill.

Okay, maybe there were no ruffled dresses or Easter suits. Maybe pastel wicker baskets have gone the way of eight-track tapes. And maybe my idea of pretty children romping through fields of clover is a bit old-fashioned.

But some things haven't changed. Kids still give us hope that the world is good—even when they're wearing smelly Batman shirts, scruffy jeans, and untied shoes. As parents, we share their joy and optimism, their promise for the future. We dare think our offspring will help make the world a better place. Heady stuff, this parenting.

I was so satisfied by the Easter egg hunt that I've gone to several since then. I anticipate the annual ritual with a sense of tingling excitement. And you never know . . . some year the park might be filled with romping children in lacy dresses and plaid bow ties.

Homemade Haircuts

Rebecca Walker Clarke

Mom always cut our hair in the kitchen if it was winter, or out on the back porch if it was warm outside. We would sit on the kitchen stool, and Mom would place masking tape straight across our bangs, then cut it off to make a nice, even line.

When I got old enough to look at my childhood photos with some degree of objectivity, I started to tease my mom about these homemade haircuts and my lack of a hairstyle, making remarks like, "I wonder where you were, Mom, the day this picture was taken? Oh, that's right, *you* got me ready!" And I vowed I'd never do anything so mean to my own children.

Now a mother myself, and faced with the reality of at least ten-dollar haircuts, I believe I can make do. I cut my daughters' hair with the barber scissors, razor, and hair cutting cape my mom gave to me. A few days ago as I cut Emme's forgivingly curly hair outside underneath our big tree, I had to wonder how old she'll be before she complains about *her* homemade haircuts.

There is only one pretty child in the world, and every mother has it.

—Chinese proverb

Picture Perfect

Rebecca Walker Clarke

My daughter Eliza's two-year-old picture was so cute that the photographer hung it on the wall in his studio. I spent a lot of money and effort on the photo, and to have my suspicions that I had an almost-perfect child confirmed by an outsider was almost too much for my mother-ego to bear. As a result, for the entire next year I had Eliza's three-year-old photo on my mind. I let her blonde hair grow out, and it got long and flipped up naturally in the back. She looked like an angel to me. I bought her a special blue dress for the upcoming three-year-old photo, and I was so taken up in the whole thing that I even periodically thought about ways she could pose.

The day before the photo shoot I walked into the bathroom to find the bottom of the tub covered in hair: chunks of blonde Eliza hair and chunks of brown Barbie hair. The little red-handled scissors were left carelessly on the bathroom rug at the scene of the crime.

I hunted Eliza down. I saw her before she saw me, and I started to shake inside: Eliza had given herself, the day before the historic event of the photo shoot, a complete chop-job. The sides of her hair were gone, as were most of her bangs.

My mind began to race: *You love her. Don't do anything foolish, Rebecca. You do love her.* But how could this happen? Other people's kids cut their hair, but not mine!

I confronted Eliza about it, and she had no shame, no remorse. I pulled out a mirror to make sure she was aware of the damage, but all she would say about it was, "It's cute, Mommy."

"You cut Barbie's hair too, Eliza. You're going to be grounded from Barbie and all her stuff for *three days.*"

I thought this was excellent. The punishment fit the crime, and this would certainly make an impression. But Eliza just ran around helping me load the box up with little plastic Barbie boots and coats and swimsuits.

There was no getting to Eliza. There was no making her believe that this new haircut was anything but a good thing. And so I put her in the bathtub and fixed her hair—sort of. After a lot of mousse and combing and a strategically placed barrette, we went ahead with the photo. It didn't turn out like I thought it would, but now it's one of my favorites.

Barbie

Heather Sundahl

My seven-month-old daughter, Georgia, had her first Barbie experience the other night. We were at a friend's house, and the little girls had hauled out the Mattel toys. Georgia was immediately transfixed by a pink plastic, convertible minivan. I know lots of women who *hate* Barbie, who loathe her waspish waist, her platinum blond corn silk hair, not to mention her trampy little shoes and micromini clothes. And I can see why some moms might want to banish Barbie and her "Made in Taiwan" bootie from their daughters' toy chests. Many of my feminist friends hate Barbie because they feel that she sends a terrible message to girls: beauty = skinny and big-chested; happiness = clothes and Ken. I admit they have a point.

Mattel, in recent years, has attempted to make Barbie more of a role model by making "Astronaut Barbie," "Dr. Barbie," "Teacher Barbie," and a host of other career-themed dolls. I, however, *love* Barbie and can't wait until Georgia is old enough to walk down that flamingo pink aisle in Toys "R" Us with me in a strange combination of desire and reverence.

Unlike many of my friends, I don't see Barbie as the devil in stilettos. I liked Barbie because she could be whatever I wanted her to be. My Barbies were superheroes, adventurers, detectives, or Olympic athletes. Okay, so I never pretended they were nuclear physicists or Rhodes scholars; that doesn't mean I didn't create fun and intelligent imaginary worlds that may or may not have contributed to my current status as a fairly interesting person. And as for Ken, Barbie's life did not revolve around that twelve-inch dude with a washboard belly and a plastic coif. For every Ken doll, we had at least four Barbie's—and no, never once did we play "Brigham Young Era Barbie," where Barbie and Skipper were sister wives to polygamist Ken. On the contrary, Ken was an accessory, like Barbie's white go-go boots or the little sombrero my aunt brought me back from Tijuana.

Although you could buy babies, my friends and I never made Barbie the mother. Was it that she seemed too young to have kids? Was it that the magenta Corvette had no room for a car seat? Certainly I was too ignorant to know that of course Barbie has never had kids because even if she managed to maintain that itty-bitty waist, no one's chest could stay *that* perky post childbearing. When I wanted to play a mom, I got out my baby dolls or played house with a friend.

But Barbie was about me, my dreams, my fantasies. Barbie was her own woman, defined neither by men nor children, changing careers like she changed those trampy shoes, free to explore and create her world. So she may not be a role model, but she sure was a lot of fun. I really do hope Georgia has a yen for dolls, because like her or not, one of these days she's getting that vacuous but fabulous friend of mine named Barbie.

They shall be mine, saith the Lord of hosts, in that day when I make up my jewels.

—Malachi 3:17

Rachel, My Jewel

Jeanne Decker Griffiths

When my first daughter was born, I imagined how close we would be and what a great mother-daughter relationship we would have. I took her to the pediatrician for the usual six-week checkup. During the exam, the doctor commented on what a stubborn baby she was. I laughed, not believing that someone's personality could be identified so early. I was wrong.

Rachel was indeed a stubborn baby who turned out to be a stubborn child. She and I spent her childhood butting heads and doing battles. I didn't know how to deal with this strong-willed little dynamo. My other children seemed so easy. I knew what they needed and could respond instinctively. Rachel was a different story. Whatever came naturally for me to do as a mother, didn't work for her. I was at a loss on how to deal with her.

When she was seven, we had another one of our confrontations. It was Mother's Day. She decided she wanted to do her own hair for church. I could just imagine what she would look like as a self-styled seven-year-old, on the stand singing with the rest of the Primary children. I offered to help. It went downhill from there.

She ended up yelling at me, "Mommy, I hate you."

I was devastated, and on Mother's Day, no less.

If she was a difficult child now, just think what she would be like as a rebellious teenager! I had nightmares of the damage she could do. I constantly prayed for help and direction, pleading, "You gave her to me, so tell me what to do!"

When she was nine, I got the answer. I was reading yet another self-help book on parenting, trying to figure out what to do. The answer jumped out from the page. The statement read: "As a parent, you need to love your child unconditionally." I felt like a ton of bricks had fallen on me. Being a good mother was important to me, so I was shocked to realize that I had unconsciously set conditions for my love. Somewhere deep inside, I had decided she didn't measure up to my expectations. The next realization was even more distressing: she knew I didn't love her unconditionally. I was absolutely heartsick.

I thought back to the time when Rachel had come home from school and happily shared with me, "My friend's name is Julie. Her mother named her that because she is her mother's jewels." Then looking up at me, with her serious blue eyes, she said, "Mommy, can I be your jewels?" That precious question was now wrenchingly painful. This innocent but ornery little child was asking me to love and treasure her, and I hadn't learned how yet, despite my best efforts.

I went back to Heavenly Father in tears. "Okay, you've given me the answer. Now please teach me how to love her unconditionally. I don't know how to do it on my own."

I made it a matter of prayer and scripture study, realizing that I was the one who needed to change. Old habits are hard to break, but day by day I made small improvements. I started to be more observant about my behavior. Amazingly, for the first time I could now see how my actions encouraged her irritation and resistance. I tried to lesson the friction and look for the positive. I bit my tongue more. I let her do her own hair, no matter what it looked like. I tried to avoid unnecessary confrontations. God slowly taught me how to love her unconditionally.

This was a child who needed a lot of emotional space, so we changed our tactics. We now tried to give clear boundaries but with as much latitude as possible, along with the unspoken message that we had confidence she would make good choices. I tried to be more supportive and respectful of those choices, even when I didn't agree with them. Fortunately, I have been blessed with a wonderful husband who is a calming influence on us all. He gave her a place of respite when she and I couldn't get along. I began to understand God's love in spite of who we are or how we act. I was most grateful when my relationship with Rachel improved, although it took a year and a half before she started to trust me.

Rachel is now a senior in high school. She is awesome. She still marches to the beat of a different drummer, but we've become accustomed to the unusual rhythm. Learning to love her unconditionally, I have grown in many ways. Despite the bumps along the way, it has been an absolute delight to see *her* blossom and grow. She is a confident, capable straight-A student, with ambitious university plans. She is committed to the gospel and hopes to go on a mission. When her friends complained about their parents, she came home and told us she couldn't think of any complaints about us. This year, more than all previous years combined, she has told me that she loves me. It's usually given as a casual passing comment. Not an overly demonstrative child, she has no idea how grateful I am each time she tells me.

When I look at Rachel, I see God's miracle. I could only offer the Lord my inadequacies, along with a willing heart. I marvel at the treasure He gave me in return. This is the child, who with Heavenly Father's help, forced me to become a better mother. And in the process, I learned to unconditionally love a remarkable young woman—Rachel, my precious jewel.

There is no way to be a perfect mother, and a million ways to be a good one.

—Jill Churchill, mystery author

Kitchen Duty
Kathryn Loosli Pritchett

My eighteen-year-old daughter, Claire, never cracked a cookbook while she lived at home. So I was delighted when, on a recent visit home from college, she told me that she'd made some "great food" for her high school pals the night before.

"Wow—how come?" I asked as I rolled out some breakfast scones.

"Well, a bunch of guys and Rachel and me were at Kurt's house, and the guys wanted to go get something to eat, but it was late and so Kurt goes, 'Hey, ladies, you want to be good moms someday. Why don't *you* go make us some food?'"

"Hmm," I said, nearly slicing my finger as I tried to cut the dough into triangles. Did Claire think this was her destiny? To cook for boys?

"Why didn't the boys just make something themselves?" I asked, flinging some cinnamon sugar on top of the scones. "Surely, they know how to run a microwave as well as you do."

"'Surely,' they do," she said.

"And that doesn't bother you that they asked you to feed them?"

"No. I cooked something for them because I wanted to."

Apparently, unlike my mother who scheduled her daily activities around meal preparation times so that my father wouldn't ever have to make his own sandwich, Claire thinks kitchen duty is an optional activity.

"Why do you think they asked you to cook for them?" I said, thinking about how the boys of my youth would never have asked us to make food for them, fearing feminist barking from us. We expected them to make their own hero sandwiches.

Claire sighed and told me that it wasn't a big deal, that it was fun to scrounge for all the stuff and make something—English muffin pizzas—out of nothing. "The boys told us we were great cooks," she added.

I thought about what she said as I took the scones out of the oven. She cooked because she wanted to; she was happy someone liked what she made. Isn't that progress?

Claire broke a scone in two, blew on it, and popped half of it into her mouth before grabbing her physics textbook off the end of the counter. "Mmm," she sighed, snagging the other half plus one more scone to take upstairs with her.

"I could teach you how to make these," I offered.

"Nah," she said. "They're great, but I've got a mid-term to study for."

Hurricane Jonah

Heather Sundahl

I think our ward needs to offer a mothering class on patience with kids going through the terrible twos (or terrible fours or eights or teens; I think all terrible stages resemble each other in some way, don't they?). I got cocky and thought that perhaps I had escaped the terrible twos with Jonah. But while Hurricane Floyd was kind of a dud here in New England, Hurricane Jonah is wreaking havoc on my sanity (but of course at church he puts on his angelic face and tricks people into believing he's sweetness personified).

One day this week I actually had to give us mutual time-outs. He flew into a rage because of something ridiculous, such as the fact that Teletubbies was over, or he couldn't find the ladder part of a fire truck. So he actually kicked me. Hard. We were in the process of changing his pants, so I whisked him up to the changing table in a less-than-tender way, and he yelled at me, "Don't do *anything* to me! ANYTHING!"

I could hardly believe my ears! Where did he get that?

When he says, "Do you want a piece of this?" and waves his fists, I know he got it from my husband's tattooed brother.

Then, as I'm changing him, he scowls at me and calls me a Man Village. He watched *The Jungle Book*, and because the boy Mogley spends the whole movie trying to avoid the Man Village, Jonah deduced that it must be a most vile and rank thing indeed. So now I'm a Man Village.

The final blow came when he said, "The whale will get you." I'm assuming since he's had the Jonah and the whale story read to him a trillion times, he thinks he's in good with the whale and can sic the big fish on his evil mama. Anyhow, we both took time-outs and afterward had a nice calm talk and hugged each other, both sorry for being so gruff.

But, sheesh. Assuming this is a stage (please, let it be a stage), when does it end? And can you wash a kid's mouth out for calling you a Man Village?

My mother had a great deal of trouble with me, but I think she enjoyed it.

—Mark Twain, humorist

Just Your Typical Mormon Family

Marci McPhee

Instant stepfamily—six kids from six to sixteen.

My four, his two.

Temple wedding.

Second marriage for us both.

We live together under the same roof for three years.

"You're not my real mother. I don't have to do what you say."

(Sigh.) "But, dear child, you *are* my real child, regardless of whether or not I bore you."

"And I am here to guide you along your life's path."

Too many teenagers, too many family dynamics.

Colliding parenting styles lead to near-explosion.

He moves out with his two kids into an apartment 1.9 miles away.

We stay very married, just working from two different bases of operation.

We talk on the phone every day; read scriptures every night as always, only by phone; go out on date night on Saturdays; take turns sleeping over at each other's houses.

After two years of that, we realize we were no closer to putting this together than we were when he first moved out.

We sell the house and buy a duplex.

He lives with his kids on one side; I live with mine on the other.

We cut a connecting door upstairs for adults only.

We run into each other in the grocery store from time to time and give the cashier something to laugh about when my husband steals a kiss as we push our separate grocery carts.

The home teachers visit us separately or together, depending on the intrafamily stress level of the day.

The kids bristle at family home evening, so we call it

"team meeting" on Monday night.

One by one, the kids grow up and leave.

When my side is empty and he is down to his last one, I move back into his side.

We patch over the connecting door.

Now the kids are all launched, and we rent out the other side.

We're into our "happily ever after" at last.

And it was well worth the wait and struggle.

Because he's just crazy about me, and I'm just crazy about him.

He's brought me a rose every Wednesday of our married lives—fifteen years and counting.

So there you have it . . . just your typical Mormon family.

"In the Quiet Heart Is Hidden . . ."

Names Withheld

There are darker aspects of motherhood in "the real world." The following comments represent concerns therapists hear in their practice.

"As an adult convert, I saw all sorts of young Mormon moms who seemed so perky and fulfilled, bouncing their babies on their knees. When I had my first child, I felt like I had been tricked, like all that cheery motherhood business was a lie. I found my previous world where I'd been confident and capable turned horribly inside out. The baby was constantly unhappy despite my best efforts and my enormous love for him. My husband was busy, grudgingly present and increasingly emotionally distant, subconsciously taking out his own 'abandonment issues' on me (we *now* know that's what was going on, but as a new parent, I had no idea what was happening). Then, when you add to that a 'have as many children as you can' mentality that was wafting in the hallways at church, I felt so depressed, miserable, incompetent, and trapped. But who could I ever admit that to?"

"You hear on the news about the 'horrid, monster parents' who shake their babies to get them to stop crying. I haven't done that. But I know the impulse. It terrifies me. Meanwhile, I go about my days looking like the happy little homemaker, leading music in Primary, buying yogurt at the grocery store."

"I have been pregnant six times. I have one child. I look around the ward and see the children who are the age my other children would have been. The grief is always there under the surface. Then, when some thoughtless person gossips about our small family, speculating on selfishness or career-driven lives, I can't decide whether I want to tear their hearts out or just go off and live in a cave somewhere."

～

"I am such an anomaly in Mormon circles. I don't really like little children. We have three and I love them all deeply, but I have no natural fondness for the task of mothering little ones. My oldest is sixteen now, and finally I'm really enjoying her (much to the amazement of my other friends with teenagers). I have hope for relating well to the other two also. Luckily, my husband is very tender and involved so that the kids weren't and aren't deprived. There's so much emphasis on the roles—mothers nurture, fathers provide— that I think fathers who have the native impulse to nurture get short shrift. And moms who don't like child rearing (but do it anyway) are viewed as somehow defective."

～

"I'm single and have no plans to marry. Still, I have the deepest longing to be a mother. I could adopt, I suppose, but I don't think I have the stamina for the social friction that would cause in my little community. So meanwhile, being childless is the thorn in my side the Apostle Paul talks about, my constant ache, my continual sorrow."

～

"Where is the place to talk about what it means to be the mother of a murderer, rapist, or other criminal? Where is the place to talk about being the daughter of a drunk, an addict, or a child abuser?"

～

"My divorce was excruciating all by itself, but watching the children suffer was the worst part of all. Everything shattered for everyone. God give us all strength to get through this."

～

"There are no adequate words to describe the agony of

watching your child in pain because of their choices—or the combination of poor choices and genetic predisposition. When your child is self-destructing—and legally, physically, and emotionally there is nothing you can do—God help you. In the end, only He can anyway. And only He really knows what you're going through."

⤙

"Yes, I'm starting to remember there is a comfort in the eternal covenants of the temple. But for the here and now, just a year after the accident where all four of my children died, I still cry every day. My well-meaning visiting teachers come and tell me it's time to cheer up, but they have no idea. No idea at all."

⤙

"Sure, being a single parent is tough. But it's better than having the kids and me get beat up."

⤙

"My twenty-eight-year-old daughter says she's happy, thriving, and glad to be free from the 'rigid thinking' of a church she 'never believed in anyway.' She's financially successful and has supportive, wonderful friends and a boyfriend she's been with for five years whom she says she'll marry when they're ready to have kids. She wants me to be happy for her. I try. But there's still something like broken glass inside me. Who thought up this agency thing? It's too hard."

⤙

"I'm a contented forty-something wife and mother. My husband and I have a merry band of four kids—ten, nine, seven, and five. These little darlings inherited my husband's blue eyes and my broad smile. Our Christmas pictures are gorgeous, if I do say so myself. But I always wonder, especially at the holidays or on his birthday, about that first son—the one I gave up for adoption twenty-two years ago. Does he have my broad smile too?"

Who knew being a mom would give such exquisite joy and such intense pain?

—Heather Sundahl, writer and humorist

Birth of a Grandmother

Marci McPhee

Friday, September 8, 2000
10:57 P.M.

My first grandchild is being born tonight.

No, I don't know whether it's a boy or a girl. Determining the gender of an unborn baby is based on ultrasounds and hospitals and doctors, not the techniques of a lay midwife who delivers babies at home. My daughter, Evelyn, will experience the drama of that moment of birth when this baby reveals the secret of its gender, the same way I found out that she was my daughter, after three sons.

11:04 P.M.

Two generations ago, I would be pacing the waiting room outside the hospital delivery room, fidgeting and mindlessly watching TV without hearing a word, waiting for the door to open with any news. Instead, tonight I'm a continent away in Boston, sitting by the cell phone, waiting for the call.

Yesterday Evelyn called me and said, "It's-me-no-baby." She said it just like that—as if it were one word that she had repeated often like a mantra to everyone she'd phoned in the last month in small-town Oregon.

Today she called me at work, at 2 P.M. Eastern time, 11 A.M. Pacific time. She said, almost shyly, "Hi, Mom." I immediately knew this was different from yesterday's call. She giggled and said her water broke. She'd called James at work, who was now racing up the mountain to be at her side. I said, "What does your midwife say?" She replied, "I guess I should call her, shouldn't I?" I was tremendously touched that she would call her husband to get home and then call me. Calling my mom was far from my mind when I went into labor. I felt so connected, so included in this time of anticipation and transition.

11:18 P.M.

Of course, I should be asleep—it's been a long day at the end of a long week—but who can sleep now? I realize there's nothing I can do from here. And staying awake doesn't help her or the baby, now on its way. But I keep watch because I cannot do otherwise. And listen for the phone to ring.

11:21 P.M.

It was not my idea to have a lay midwife attend the birth, half an hour from the closest convenience store, much less hospital, in the remote woods of Oregon. I never sent the seven-page letter I wrote, trying to talk her out of it. Childbirth *is* "the valley of the shadow of death." And I know too many casualties and near-casualties. But she was undaunted—and I, just learning how to be the mother of a grown daughter, kept my opinions to myself. Just as I've kept my opinions to myself about their whole "timeless" lifestyle, living without watches or clocks. "When the first rays of the sun hit the maple tree above the second branch, it's time to go to work." I've also kept my opinions to myself about their names for the baby—all Latin botanical names for species of trees.

So now, I do the only thing I can do—pray for guardian angels to assist her and the baby as they pass through the valley of the shadow of death, that it may be a safe transition for them both. And I send her positive energy and . . . luck.

11:25 P.M.

What an unexpected blessing—to be sharing my own transition into grandmotherhood with my only daughter, the youngest of four children. It would be so much different if it were one of the boys making me a grandmother. Instead, Evelyn and I shared our initial feelings of shock about the pregnancy (for both of us), anxiety about what to do now, and the settling-in adjustments, each from our own perspective. We've also shared tender moments, talking about pregnancy and delivery and breast-feeding and diapering, shopping for maternity clothes together. I'm so glad I'm able to share with her my own swirling jumble of mixed emotions about all that this pregnancy means to both of us.

11:46 P.M.

While birthing my own children, I was obviously very wrapped up in the process itself. Now, a generation removed from contractions and labor pains, I have the luxury of thinking about this from another perspective: I wonder what it's like in the premortal life right now, at this time of birth? Is this child having a going-away party? Is it a surprise party? Farewell "until-we-meet-again" hugs for dear friends, family members, and perhaps a future soul mate and eternal companion? Does the spirit watch its own birth? Is there a birth canal that must be traversed from that celestial realm to this, with its own life-changing transition process? Are there final instructions upon departing one's first existence? Or perhaps a Father's blessing?

This baby leaves a celestial world filled with love where all is light and enters this mortal world where many loving family members and friends have been sent ahead to welcome this dear child to this new world. I fiercely count myself as one of them—and pledge myself to staunchly love this baby, guard and protect this baby with all my strength, and accept this baby with all my heart. I know none of us will ever be the same after tonight.

Thuja Amber Wood was born September 9, 2000, at sunset sharp. Mother, daughter, and Grammy are doing fine.

Baby Names

Heather Sundahl

How much of this is "the terrible twos" and how much is related to the impending arrival of a sibling? On the surface Jonah seems happy at the prospect of a sister. He kisses little babies and loves to read all the *I'm a Big Brother Now* books I've bought or checked out from the library. But I'm getting hints at some deep-rooted resentment and anxiety about the new baby. For example, about six weeks ago I asked Jonah what we should name the baby.

"Garlic," was his reply.

Okay. Kinda quirky and funny.

A week or so later when I asked again, he replied, "The baby's name is Stinky."

Seeing a pattern emerge? And then three weeks ago, he spontaneously informed me that the baby's name is Skunk and pointed at my belly and yelled, "Ew Pew!" as he ran away from me.

This week he's gone back to Garlic, which I find the best of the bunch.

But I don't know which is more challenging—dealing with a wacky two-year-old or trying to come up with a name Dave and I both like. We've been through *2001 Baby Names, Beyond Jennifer and Jason,* and a couple of really big family histories with names going back to the third century in Scotland and still are stumped. I've even taken to clicking through the soaps on occasion but keep running into names like Raven, which I can't picture myself yelling in the park someday ("Raven, come let Mama wipe your nose!").

We are currently in the denial mode and have taken to calling my belly Garlic, which seems to please Jonah. Garlic is powerful stuff.

Who doesn't love garlic bread, and if there's a werewolf around, garlic's your root of choice, right?

There are worse names, aren't there?

Garlic is as good as ten mothers.

—Indian proverb

Up and Down and All Around

Judith Harding

Fertility treatment was like riding the surf—a heady rise in the air followed by the crash of a wave. For three years we lived in the same up-and-down cycle with calendars, blood tests, and horse-sized needles followed by a "nope, you're not pregnant" report by telephone. Inevitable tears.

It seemed that I would never be able to give up trying to get pregnant. I guess it's a lot like gambling with slot machines. Maybe this time will be the jackpot. . . . We are blessed to live in a state in which treatment is paid for by insurance, allowing for many in vitro fertilization trials. While actively engaged in fertility treatment, some people suggested that we should begin the adoption process simultaneously. Although this dual effort is not recommended by professionals, it seems that many couples make the attempt. However, I could not juggle fertility appointments, adoption efforts, work, and the rest of life all at once. It was surprisingly exhausting.

After three years, one day I realized that I was done with the Lupron, IVF doctors, and Pergonal. My husband had long since tired of his lonely part of the process. Hey, after all those years of singlehood, I thought making babies was supposed to be fun! Unfortunately, fertility treatment can lack a certain *joie-de-vivre* and spontaneity, decreasing all-around appeal for everyone involved.

So on to adoption, which had to be easier, right? There, at last, we could be more in control of our destiny. Of course, it was not easy at all. There were endless false starts and dead ends. The number of sources I tried during those next years leaves me breathless. I called every adoption source I could find, from LDS Social Services to fundamentalist Christian groups to adoption lawyers. We were too old or too "Mormon sect" or too poor ($25,000 to $30,000!) to be successful. Well, I'm not easily deterred, so I sent letters to almost everyone we knew regarding our desires, with letters for them to pass on. We joined groups and placed expensive newspaper ads across the country. When we went to the movies, I looked around for people to talk to—wanting to ask if anyone might know a family who wanted to give up a baby for adoption. At one desperate moment, I considered dropping thousands of contact cards over Boston from an airplane. Surely something would work.

Three years later I attended a professional workshop outside of Toronto, Ontario, Canada. When I met one of the participants, who happened to be a former colleague of my husband, I made my very familiar statement, "We are hoping to adopt. Do you know anyone who is looking for an adoptive couple?" He said, "Well, yes. I do." After all that time, I could hardly believe it was a possibility!

We had many phone calls with the birth parents, some uncertain. Happily, when I went out to meet them, everything went well. The birth mom was so clear about this decision, the birth dad less so. She told us when to fly out for the baby's birth, and we did.

Indeed, the birth parents called on the way to the hospital for the delivery. Like them, we rushed to the hospital for the birth. When we went into her room, there they were with this little purple round ball of a baby. It was an extremely tender moment with two sets of parents and one new baby boy.

We watched him weighed, bathed, and swaddled. Oh, so new and yet quite big, compared to his peers in the nursery. What a miracle of life he was. In the days that followed, we snuggled, laughed, cried, and hardly slept. So *this* is motherhood!

All the interactions among birth and adoptive family and

friends were gentle and tentative over the next four days. The baby had an irregular heartbeat, so he had to remain in the hospital. The birth mom was having her tubes tied, so she was there too. The nurses and doctor felt caught in the middle between the two factions and seemed resentful of us, in fact. That was hard but understandable too. Birth siblings of each parent came to see the baby, as well as other family members. Meanwhile, our family and friends poured into the hospital for a look at this long-waited-for, sweet baby. He stayed with us (we had a room at the hospital) but also visited birth family members in the mom's room. We went over to see them too.

The most poignant moment, perhaps, was the departure from the hospital. Two of our dearest friends watched the final good-byes from the birth parents, with tears all around as we left the hospital. We felt such joy and gratitude for this sweet baby boy and such sorrow for them in their loss.

After a day to settle in with close friends, my husband left to return to work at home while I remained the requisite week in the state. Two days after we left the hospital, the birth mom called. That was not in the plan the birth mom and I had made. "Do you think the pain will ever go away?" she asked. Two mothers, two fathers, one baby. I said, "Probably some, not all. You have to do whatever you think is the right thing to do. All I ask is that you get clear, really clear. Then let us know."

The baby and I stayed with our dear friends in the interim. I decided this might be the only time I would have a sweet little one to love, so I'd enjoy every minute. Each night I stayed up to hold and watch him. I would talk to him and tell him how loved he was. My friend, the mother of eight, taught me how to bathe him without dropping him in the sink. Her hands moved with assurance and ease. Ah, the comfort of practice and familiarity!

One night about 11:30, the phone rang. I answered, and it was the birth mother and father. They said they had made the decision. I knew and had known all week their answer— they would take the baby back. I braced myself and loved them for how hard it must've been to decide what to do. The mom said something, but I could not quite hear her.

"I beg your pardon?" I offered.

"We want you to keep him," she said.

Silence. Disbelief.

"Are you sure? You must do the right thing for both you and him."

"Yes, we are sure."

And so it was. Sweet baby Jesse was transferred from one set of parents to another. Motherhood had come to me, but not without its price to the mother and father who gave him life.

Biology is the least of what makes someone a mother.

—Oprah Winfrey

The Accessory

Judith Harding

We were about to adopt a child. I wanted this child's life to begin as much as possible in the way I had always planned. That meant breast-feeding, and from my reading and discussing with La Leche League members, even an adoptive mother could do it—with effort. I was certainly prepared to give it my best.

First step: Get a breast pump. Not a wimpy handheld one, you understand—a big, heavy electric one. It is important to know that with adoption you haven't really had nine months to plan your life. So, in the month before the baby's birth, I had a lot to do. I was one of the codirectors for girls' camp, was helping my mother pack up and move from California to Utah, and was still working full time and had three teenage stepchildren at home.

However, La Leche League instructions were clear: If you want to be successful, you must pump daily for about thirty minutes. Picture me at girls' camp in the leaders' cabin. Each day I am modestly attempting my afternoon pump when various pairs and groups of girls walk in to chat. My own compadres are holding back the laughter at such a novice's out-of-place effort with young, impressionable girls about.

Then, in order to get to California to help my mom, I had to fly—and not a direct flight at that. This oh-so-heavy pump was not something to be stuffed in a suitcase. No, it had to be held and carried through the various security gates at each airport. At one stop in Dallas, the older security agent asked, "What is it?"

"A breast pump," I quietly replied.

"What?" he asked again, louder.

"A breast pump," I ventured, a little louder this time.

"What?" he yelled.

"A breast pump!" I yelled.
People turned and looked.
I blushed.
But, I suppose, that's nothing compared to childbirth. . . .

Images of Motherhood

Harriet P. Bushman

Wading through the indescribable mess of three teen-agers' bedrooms—

Finding a by-now-blue-and-furry cookie hurled moons ago (in abandon—or rage) behind a bookcase—

Valiantly fighting—occasionally losing—the battle to stay awake as a late arrival describes in precise detail a film just seen–

This is all part of the fabulous challenge of motherhood.

Was my own mother ever thus challenged?

How is it that I scarcely remember beyond the sunlit afternoons in the garden

And the crowds for Sunday lunch

And lying at opposite ends of the bathtub together chatting and confiding until I was almost twenty?

Was I one of the extraordinarily fortunate ones to have been born friends with my mother—a friendship never to change until I embraced a religion beyond her understanding?

Thankfully that change was eventually absorbed.

New and deeper bonds have been forged as my own status changed to mother.

I remember how she used to deal with many of the situations I face daily.

It makes me smile and feel encouraged, because her heart was always so light with the enjoyment of life, with laughing and finding the brightness and fun in everything.

Now, long vacations idle by at her seaside house where, to the sound of the waves, we sit by candlelight for leisurely, conversation-filled dinners, eating the homegrown food my mother, at nearly eighty, still loves to provide.

It is prior to these daily feasts, framed in the gateway to

her greenhouses and neat rows of summer plenty, that I do and will always think of her—

Hair flying, shaggy dog at her feet, arms filled with baskets of peaches and figs and the succulent, tender vegetables for building new generations of healthy bodies, never forgetting, as summer closes in, tart green apples for pies.

Actions Speak

Suzanne Midori Hanna

Although she wears a ring from Yugoslavia inscribed with the word *Love*, I don't remember Mother ever telling me in words to love my neighbor. The delicious and plentiful food she gave to others was matched only by the heroics of her compassion. Take the day we went to see Maggie Johns. Mom had a "feeling" that everything wasn't quite right. She asked me to come along. The plan was to go under the ruse of visiting Maggie and Hal's new house. I was eagerly waiting to get my learner's permit, so Mom had to drive. Good thing!

We didn't know the term "battered woman" back in those days, but when we saw her bruised face, we didn't need words. When the phone rang and Hal went to answer, Maggie clutched her baby, and we all raced to the car and locked the doors.

Before we got away, Hal came running, jumping on the hood, pounding the windshield and screaming, "Peggy Hanna, don't take my wife! Peggy Hanna!"

By then, Mom was in reverse, swinging her trusty 1966 Mustang into the street.

"Lay a patch, Mom!" I yelled.

Hal slid off as we sped home.

Mom's boldness on behalf of others was always a way of life. At fifteen I didn't know there was any other way to be. It never dawned on me that she was teaching me to love my neighbor, take action when needed, and never "shrink or shun the fight."

Feed My Sheep

Laurel Madsen

She was short—just five feet tall and ninety pounds at her marriage, she told us once—rather more than "pleasingly plump" during my childhood and youth, and back to a frail ninety pounds in the last years of her life. Her feet were swift to serve others; she had boundless energy until illness took it from her; she laughed a lot; she loved picnics, ice-cold root beer, pretty clothes and silly hats, and flowers—oh, how she loved flowers! She adored her husband and children—and the in-law children and grandkids when they took their places in her family—and they adored her in return. She liked just about everybody she met. She was gentle and sweet—couldn't bear quarrels and confrontation and simply was unable to stand up for herself or her children when perhaps there were times she should have.

That was my mom.

I was born to her when she was forty-four, the last of her nine children, but I didn't realize that she was an older mother until someone pointed it out when I was rather a big kid. Her gaiety and liveliness made our household a fun place to be. I remember sitting with a bunch of girlfriends around a tablecloth spread on the floor, while we ate our fill of feather-light, dollar-sized baking powder biscuits with butter and jam.

As a farm wife with a huge garden and raspberry patch, working crews to feed, and canning to be done, she didn't often have time to read to me. But she told me stories—magical stories—as I played nearby while she worked. And she sang to me in her high, off-key voice. Outside, she sang my name in the cadence of the meadowlark, carefully pulled aside branches of the raspberry bush to show me a miniature nest with eggs the size of marbles in it, put my hesitant hand on a calf's nose, and pointed out elephants and tigers in the cloud formations of the sky.

Mother's guiding principle of life was kindness—thinking always of the other person's feelings. She didn't preach it; I just observed it as she offered friendship to the Navaho Indian women who came to work on our farm, as she served a plate of hot food to a tramp who stopped at her door, as she put her arms around anyone who needed comfort. And she taught me in just a few, matter-of-fact words. Once I told her that two of my friends said they wouldn't come to my birthday party if I invited a certain unpopular girl. "Well, we'll miss them," she said, and that was that. In my teenage years a girl wrote a malicious letter to me, and I composed a nasty reply; I was quite proud of it. Mom read it over. "Do you really want to be like her?" was the only comment she made, and it was enough.

My mother died when I was only twenty-five, and that's been a lot of years ago, but I think of her nearly every day. When I turn back the sheets and blankets and open the window so that the bed can "air" before I make it, when I crack an egg on the side of the bowl and skillfully pour the white and yolk back and forth in the shell halves to separate them, or when I ladle hot fruit into canning jars, I think of her and smile. She taught me to do those things.

But most of all, she taught me to be kind. The stake president spoke at her funeral and told us about Jesus instructing Peter three times to "feed my sheep." Looking down into the faces of her grieving children, dear Brother Edgley gently told us that when we remembered our mother we should think of those words: "feed my sheep." I always have, and when I try to live up to them, I know that my mother is smiling.

Peace of Cake

Suzanne Midori Hanna

I'm making a birthday cake for my mom: Inez Borg's Orange Sponge Cake with Chocolate Whipped Cream Icing! She made this delicacy every year when we were kids. I remind her of this, but she no longer remembers all the many things she has done for many people over her many years. She is now eighty-five and lives with me. Parkinson's, rheumatoid arthritis, osteoporosis, and dementia have left her helpless. People see me pushing her wheelchair and they say, "You're a wonderful daughter!" I reply, "Really, it's she who's a wonderful *mother!*"

But I do wonder, "Why is this only the first time in my fifty-three years that I have made Inez Borg's Orange Sponge Cake with Chocolate Whipped Cream Icing?" I know the answer. The cake is my way of celebrating the whole woman. It is a sign of the peace that has come between us as the years brought her a daughter who became a Democrat while she was Republican, a career woman while she was a homemaker, and a fast-food junkie while she was a gourmet cook. Through all these developments, we rocked back and forth with the winds of life until we found a way to live with these differences. When I got into my thirties, I remember thinking that something had changed, and now Mother was my favorite houseguest, easy and enjoyable to have around. Who would have thought we were being prepared for this stage of our lives?

The making of this cake is also a sign that she can't do it, and if some traditions are to continue, someone has to pick up the ball. As the only daughter, I am that someone. Now, I give her this cake as a token of all the things she taught me.

My Mother's Advice

Mette Harrison

I was born the ninth of eleven children, when my mother was forty years old. I often felt like we were more than two generations removed. She didn't give advice often, but this was what she had to say about fashion:

Never wear blue and green together.

Don't wear white shoes until Memorial Day and not after Labor Day.

Always wear lipstick to church.

Everything coordinates with red.

If it has wear left in it, it stays in your closet.

If it's cheap, it's a good deal.

Never wear white pants.

On the other hand, maybe her other advice is more enduring:

When your husband moves, go with him.

When your baby cries, don't go immediately to pick her up.

There's always room on the wall for another family photo.

Sleep when you can.

A little cream never hurt anyone.

A good book is the best dessert.

Always keep some candy in your purse.

Walking around the block a few times keeps anyone fit.

If the garbage needs to be taken out, take it out yourself.

Keep serving the leftovers until they're gone.

Never get sick.

Keep your hands busy.

Don't be in a hurry to get married.

Just because it's new and improved doesn't mean it's better.

Go barefoot.

I hope my advice is as good—and as amusing, twenty years later—to my kids.

Blood Pressure

Nancy Harward

Earlier this year, I went to the doctor for a long-overdue physical, motivated by a concern that I sometimes became light-headed during my menstrual periods. After determining that my weight, cholesterol level, and blood sugar all were within normal ranges, and that my heart rate was that of a marathon runner (which I'm not), the doctor informed me that I was, "if anything, *too* healthy."

"Then why the light-headedness?" I asked.

"You have really low blood pressure," she explained. "Apparently, that's normal for you; but fluid loss during your periods may cause it to drop enough to make you feel faint. Eat more salt so you can retain more fluids."

On the way home from the doctor's office, I considered the irony of being diagnosed with abnormally low blood pressure during a phase of my life when I felt abnormally stressed out. In addition to trying to attend—if not set up for and clean up after—the torrent of concerts, recitals, athletic events, awards banquets, and graduation parties that occur toward the end of every school year, I was also working extra hours at two part-time jobs, organizing a bi-stake Young Women camp, and preparing for my daughter's wedding.

Clearly, I had inherited neither my mother's metabolism nor her disposition. Mom was a high-energy, type-A personality who could "fly off the handle" (a phrase she liked to use) over something as simple as her once-a-month Relief Society lesson or the fact that no one had vacuumed the living room when guests were about to arrive.

"Mom, calm down!" my sister would say. "If you don't, you're going to die of a popped heart!"

My sister was only half joking. When Mom was in her

early forties, she came home from a routine check-up, having been diagnosed with both high blood pressure and diabetes, and she was sure she was going to die. Although it would be another thirty years before she actually did, Mom lived the rest of her life as if each day were her last chance to direct the affairs of the world.

When Mom discovered that she was having another child, she was not happy, and she resented the fact that my father greeted the news with obvious delight.

"Ned, that's wonderful!" he had said.

"No, it's not!" she had retorted.

Mom must have felt that she had already contributed her share to the post-war baby boom, having given birth to three girls between 1947 and 1950. By 1955, when the third and most rambunctious of her daughters was about to start school, she must have been looking forward to the few hours of R&R that kindergarten might afford. But then I came along.

To her credit, Mom never made me feel like an imposition. On the contrary, I always felt that I was the most cherished of her children. I was the one who got her undivided attention while my sisters were at school, the one who accompanied her everywhere she went for the first five years of my life—and beyond. Not long after I began first grade, I again ruined my mother's opportunity for time to herself by contracting a series of infections that kept me out of school during most of the next two years. I wasn't exactly sick all that time; I just needed to stay away from other children with snotty noses and sticky hands. So my mother remained my primary playmate—which was fine, except that Mom wasn't very good at playing. She was a lot more comfortable getting things done.

Although I had a closet full of games and an extensive collection of Barbie paraphernalia, I don't remember playing much during the months I spent sequestered from other kids. Instead, I shadowed my mother as she went about her daily activities: fixing meals, washing dishes, folding laundry, baking cookies, running errands. Watching and sometimes helping, I learned to knead bread, make soup from scratch, mend clothing, run a ditto machine, choose a good pineapple, and hunt for bargains.

As I watched her rip out rows and rows of her knitting to fix one misplaced stitch, and later, as I watched her raise a disapproving eyebrow over misplaced stitches in my own knitting, I eventually learned to be critical, to be demanding, to settle for nothing less than the best. My mother set high standards and expected her children to meet them. The pressure was on.

By the time I graduated from high school, Mom and I had become very close, but the differences in our personalities had become more pronounced. She was gregarious; I was reserved. She loved to argue; I hated disagreements. She acted quickly and decisively; I was slow and deliberate. (I had, in fact, become a lot more like my dad—even though he and I never spent much time together. But that's another story.) I looked up to my mother and wanted her to be proud of me, but sometimes our personality differences got in the way of mutual appreciation.

The most serious, stressful issue to come between us was my choice of a husband. Mom didn't exactly disapprove of Michael, and she didn't exactly dislike him. She just didn't know exactly what to make of him. Michael and I had met and courted while I was away at college, so although by the time we got married, my parents had at least become acquainted with him, they didn't really know him. After the wedding, Mom began to learn that, unlike her other sons-in-law, Michael would neither argue nor kowtow to her; rather, he would listen politely to her demands and then do exactly as he wished. I don't think she had ever encountered someone like him: someone she couldn't control.

Moreover, Mom must have felt that I too was now beyond her sphere of influence. As married children inevitably do, I had transferred my primary loyalties from parents to spouse, and I think that was hard for her to take. In addition, a hidden wedge had been placed between my mother and me that would take years to discover and dislodge.

On our wedding day, Michael and I had driven to the temple together, assuming that our parents would be following shortly in their own cars. Michael's mother arrived and began helping me dress; my mother, chronically late, had not appeared by the time the matron was ready to begin the traditional pre-endowment meeting with the brides-to-be and their female escorts. Reluctant to keep everyone else waiting, Michael's mom and I went on into the meeting, where concerns about my own mother's whereabouts kept me from concentrating on the matron's message.

At some point during her presentation, the door I had been anxiously watching opened, but it wasn't my mother who came through it. Instead, an elderly temple worker approached me and whispered, "Do you have someone with you?" Because the woman who was about to become my mother-in-law was seated beside me, I answered, "Yes." It didn't occur to me to ask the worker if she knew what had happened to my mom.

When the meeting was over, I was greatly relieved to find my mother waiting in the hall outside, and we continued together into the endowment room. Too overwhelmed by my own emotions to notice anyone else's that day, I failed to recognize that my mother did not seem as elated as she should have been to see her youngest daughter married in the temple. It wasn't until a few days later, when Michael and I returned from our honeymoon to pack up our wedding gifts and head back to school, that I sensed a distinct chill in my mother's demeanor. In fact, she was downright nasty to us, speaking in clipped sentences and dispensing only the stiffest of hugs before we drove away.

For the next several months, I assumed that my mother's coldness toward both of us was due to her discomfort with Michael and also, perhaps, to a reluctance to accept the fact that her days of active parenting were over. I told myself that things would get better as time went on, but they didn't. Years passed. We moved across the country. My mother and I continued to write, call, and visit each other as often as possible, and though we managed to converse and even laugh together, our exchanges were never as warm as they once had been.

Actually, some of our exchanges were pretty heated. As I mentioned earlier, Mom loved to argue; and although I disliked being dragged into a debate, I often felt the need to defend my husband from her disparagement. She sniffed at his small-town upbringing, scoffed at his opinions, and belittled his accomplishments. When we began having children, she criticized his parenting methods. Mom rarely aimed her darts directly at me, but because I was caught between her and Michael, I took most of the hits. It hurt, but it seemed fair: after all, I was the one who had chosen this imperfect young man as her son-in-law.

Hoping to regain my mother's favor but knowing that I couldn't change Michael, I attempted to refashion myself into what I thought was her image of a good wife, mother, and daughter. I lost weight. I changed my hairstyle (something Mom had been trying to get me to do since junior high). I prepared exceptional meals and kept the kitchen clean. I made curtains for the house and clothes for the kids. I took my children to the library regularly and tried to stay well informed myself. No matter what I did, however, it never seemed to be enough. Mom continued to criticize, and her praise was faint. And even though she rarely did it overtly, I always thought I saw one eyebrow raised in disapproval whenever she came to visit.

Then, after several years of mounting frustration, things began to change. One evening while we were visiting my parents in California, I unexpectedly discovered the wedge that had begun to sunder my relationship with my mother the day I was married. Mom had planned a family cookout at the beach where Michael and I had gone on our honeymoon. After dinner, as we reminisced together about our wedding, my mother made a startling disclosure.

"That was one of the most difficult days of my life," she said. "It really hurt to know that you didn't want me to be your escort at the temple."

"What do you mean?" I asked, stunned.

"Remember? I had to wait in the hall by myself while you and Mike's mother went to the bride's meeting," she explained.

"But, Mom," I exclaimed, "you weren't there! We waited for you as long as we could, but the matron decided to go ahead and start. I kept hoping you would come in, but you never did."

"I was a few minutes late and wasn't sure where they had taken you," she said. "I went to the worker at the desk and found out that the bride's meeting had already started. I tried to explain that my daughter was getting married and that I was supposed to be in the meeting with her. I gave her your name, but she still didn't seem to understand and wouldn't open the door for me—you know how temple workers can be. Finally, she agreed to go in to see if you were in the meeting. When she came back, she said, 'She said she already has someone with her.' Then she pointed to a chair and told me to wait there until you came out."

I gaped at her, so taken aback that I couldn't think of anything to say.

"How do you think I felt to hear that my own daughter didn't want me to be with her in the temple?" Mom went on. "How do think I felt to hear that you wanted your husband's mother to be with you instead of me?"

"Oh, Mom!" I cried. "That's not what I wanted at all! Of course I wanted you to be there! I was so busy wondering where you were that I couldn't even pay attention to what the matron was saying. I had no idea you were out in the hall!"

"But didn't the worker tell you I was there? Why did you tell her that you already had someone with you?"

Confused, I struggled to recall exactly what had happened. Suddenly it all came back, and I remembered the worker whispering to me. She had asked, "Do you have someone with you?" and I had replied, "Yes." She had never mentioned the fact that my mother was waiting alone in the hall.

With that misunderstanding resolved, my mother and I found that we could talk to each other again without feeling that we were walking across thin ice. Living on opposite sides of the country, we didn't meet often, and when we did, she was as demanding and critical as ever, but I guess I learned to accept the fact that that's just the way she was. I guess I also learned to accept the fact that I was who I was and that trying to become someone different just to please my mother wasn't going to make either of us happy. She learned to accept me as I am, also coming to appreciate the idea that I could live happily and successfully without being as driven as she.

Equally important to me, Mom eventually learned to accept and appreciate Michael. Some years after my mother and I began to reconcile our differences, Michael was asked to attend a convention held very near my parents' home. Mom and Dad had had few opportunities to see their eastern-born grandchildren, so Michael asked if they would like him to bring our two preschoolers along on his business trip. They could travel for half price, and their absence from home would give me some much needed time to myself while our older children were at school. With some trepidation my parents said yes to the plan, agreeing to keep the toddlers during the day while Michael attended meetings.

Watching him interact with our children when he returned to their home each evening that week, my parents had a chance to see my husband the way I saw him: as a loving, capable, involved father. Talking with him after he put the kids to bed, they enjoyed his intelligent conversation and wit, and they recognized his love for me. After that trip my mother finally began to treat Michael as something other than an adversary.

Only a few months later, Mom became seriously ill. This time she was diagnosed with cancer, and although the doctor's prognosis was hopeful, we all knew that she didn't have another thirty years to direct the affairs of the world. Still living on the east coast and tied there by a limited budget and a house full of kids, I couldn't do much to ease her pain or help her and Dad keep their household running.

About a year and a half after Mom's cancer treatments began, Michael and I scraped together enough money for a plane ticket so I could join my sisters in a visit to Mom and Dad. It had been years since all of us had been together, and it was the first time ever that we'd all been back at home without any husbands or children. It was slightly unnerving to see ourselves reverting to the patterns we'd established in childhood—everybody treated me like the little sister again—but it was even more unnerving to see Mom stripped of her characteristic energy. For the first time in our lives, Mom actually needed us to do things for her. Remembering the days, weeks, and months she had spent caring for me when I was sick, cleaning up my vomit, helping me sip 7Up through a flex straw, and applying cool, wet cloths to my fevered forehead, I was grateful for the chance to return the favor, even for a few days.

The following spring, when Michael's boss assigned him to attend another convention in California, we decided to dip into our savings and turn his trip into a family vacation. Although Mom was between treatments and had been feeling pretty well, we thought it best not to stay at the house with all our vivacious children, so we interspersed visits to Mom's bedside with trips to a neighborhood playground, the hotel pool, and Disneyland. At first, the kids were a little wary of the bald, emaciated woman lying in Grandma's bed, but gradually they warmed up to her, playing card games, answering her questions about their interests, and enjoying her undiminished ability to tell a good story.

On our last afternoon there, when the convention had ended early and Michael had taken the kids to the playground, Mom and I had a chance to talk without interruptions. We recalled good times, discussed old friends and my sisters and their families, and then the topic of conversation turned to my husband.

"You know, you really got the best of the lot," my mother said. "Mike is a wonderful father." She proceeded to enumerate many other qualities that she admired in him and ended by saying, "How blessed you are to have found such a great man."

Six weeks after we left California, my oldest sister called to tell me that Mom was back in the hospital. An hour and a half later, she called again. Mom had died. How blessed I felt to have had those last moments with her, to see my children laughing and playing with her, to know that she not only approved of my husband, but considered him a great man. I grieved but felt at peace.

More than a dozen years have gone by. I now have a son-in-law of my own, and my youngest daughter is about to graduate from high school. She and her siblings think I am demanding and critical, that I set impossibly high standards for them. I admit that I occasionally raise a disapproving eyebrow when they offer less than their best. But they have no idea how much harder it could be. They've never had to live with someone who has high blood pressure.

There are only two things a child will share willingly: communicable diseases and his mother's age.

—Dr. Benjamin Spock, pediatrician

Flu

Heather Sundahl

The stomach flu descended on our household this week with a vengeance. The only thing worse than sick kids is a sick mom . . . with sick kids and a sick husband. Just once I want the privilege of being sick all by myself with no one else for me to worry about. I can't believe I now look back wistfully to times when I was single and sick and could lie on the couch drinking ginger ale, watching a *non*-Disney movie or rush to the bathroom and not have a little fist pounding on the door shouting, "Mama, I *need* your privacy! Let me in!"

Grave Circumstances

E. Victoria Grover

My father was the flashy star of our family. He fled his sad childhood into a life of hard work, ambition, and success, and even after his death at age sixty-three, my mother, three older sisters, and I continued to place him squarely at the center of our family. He died after only a few months of illness and had provided for us financially but had made no funeral arrangements at all. In the days immediately after his death, we five women went everywhere together, selecting a funeral home, finding a cemetery, and making all the necessary arrangements.

While we had not really anticipated this job, my sisters and I knew we could figure out the funeral business if we had to. My father died in 1970, and we grew up into independent, assertive, and self-confident adults. Three out of four of us were either in or working toward professional lives, in addition to our lives as wives and mothers, and if you had asked us at the time, I think we each would have attributed our accomplishments to our father's shining example.

Our mother, after all, was a wonderful person, but she was also a quiet, stay-at-home wife who never even went to college and blended comfortably in to the background of our family portrait. Now, with our father gone, we four daughters stepped forward and took turns helping our sheltered mother cope with this calamity. She was calm but stunned with grief, and she clearly valued our assistance. She asked us questions before she made any decisions, listening carefully and appreciatively to our answers. She took time to ponder what we said; then she acted, and somehow we pushed through each crazy day.

We finally found a cemetery we all liked, and the plot my mother bought was a double plot meant to hold the remains of both my father and eventually my mother. It came with one large headstone. As days went by and the reality of my father's death sank in, our grief deepened. The funeral had not helped us very much.

After the ceremony my mother asked us to plan the inscription for the gravestone, and we struggled to put some of our loss into the words that would be carved upon that stone. First, we mapped out our father's name in large letters across the top. Then beneath his name, in letters almost as large, we wrote the government title that was the symbol of his life's achievement. Under that we wrote the dates of his birth and death, and finally we added a long (two whole lines!) epitaph fitting for this great man who had left such an enormous hole in our world.

Our final design seemed to us to illuminate the whole face of the headstone. It shouted out the natural and right reasons for our enormous grief. We felt better just looking at it. We showed it triumphantly to my mother, who studied it for a few minutes, then told us it was "perfect." She thanked us, again admiring the work of her "multitalented daughters," and the carving of the stone was commissioned. In the next few months, despite our busy lives, we each found time individually to visit my father's grave. The beautifully engraved stone we had designed together was always a great comfort to us as we came alone to place new flowers or take old ones away.

It wasn't until about a year later that all five of us could be together once more at the graveside. On that day my mother was planting two small shrubs beside the headstone. While the rest of us worked on the plantings, one of my sisters wandered over to look at the new headstone of a nearby freshly dug grave. Suddenly she looked at my father's stone and gasped! We all looked up at her as she pointed first at the new stone, which was clearly still half empty, awaiting the identifying information of a still-living spouse, then pointed back to our own beloved gravestone.

"What about *Mom*?" she cried.

Before that moment I don't believe any of us kids realized the future dilemma we had created. There was simply no room on the face of our double plot gravestone for any information about our mother! We turned to her as she sat back on her knees with a small trowel in one hand, apparently to think about this new turn of events. She looked calm as usual, but she had a quirky little smile on her face that let us know this news was *not* a surprise to her.

With genuine distress and a little exasperation (her calm bemusement in the face of apparently serious problems had sometimes driven my father crazy too), we asked her, "So, what will we do when *you* die?"

"Well," my mother said, her smile growing broader. She pointed helpfully at the raised concrete base on which the large stone was set.

"I've thought about that. I think you should just put a little plaque on the bottom here that says 'and wife.'"

In the dead silence that followed her suggestion, she began to laugh. In a few moments the absurdity of our dilemma dawned on us all, and we joined her with some rather rueful laughter of our own. A long-standing family joke was born.

We've since come up with many different suggestions about where and how to acknowledge Mom's place in the cemetery after her death (my favorite involves flashing neon tubing). She listens to them all attentively. Sometimes she laughs at the marvelous wit of her four daughters. But she absolutely refuses to tell us what to do. As far as she is concerned, her children created the problem, and therefore they will eventually have to find the solution, and by eventually, she means when she is no longer around to either confirm or deny the wisdom of it. She looks us each in the eye and tells us she is confident we will find a good solution.

Since we were first able to talk, she has listened soberly to our ideas—about gravestones, about school and work, about our families, about dinner for next Thanksgiving, about politics and peace and justice in the world. Sometimes she'd ask questions, suggest different viewpoints, and even point out problems with our proposals. When we'd sorrowfully admit our mistakes, she would reiterate her conviction that mistakes are inevitable and often even useful, and then she'd laugh and show us not to be afraid of mistakes—the same way she showed us not to be afraid of monsters in the dark.

I wonder if my wise and illustrious father really was the source of his daughter's self-confident achievements. My mother was just "the usual mom," very strict when we were young children, requiring polite and considerate behavior from her daughters at almost all times. She knew how to "reprove betimes with sharpness," but she also made great chocolate chip cookies for us and the whole neighborhood. And she had a way of looking directly into our eyes whenever we spoke, even when we were very little, so that we knew she was listening carefully to what we said. The older we got, the more often she solemnly accepted the validity of our words and ideas, even if sometimes she then added that she didn't agree with them and was not going to allow us to act on them.

Somehow over the years of our adolescence, she managed to slowly transfer the rights and responsibilities of judgment and choosing from herself to each one of us. I have no idea how she did it, but I do know that by the time we were young adults she simply refused to make any of our decisions for us. Usually she would not even *hint* at what she *might think* we should do! She seemed genuinely relieved to no longer have that difficult job, to at last only be accountable for her own choices. She continued to express her faith that we were fully capable of figuring out a solution to whatever problems beset us and acting on our decisions, without any help from her.

My mother is almost ninety-one, and she still won't tell us what to do about that gravestone. When the time comes, she says, we'll figure something out. I think she's right. And I also think that maybe you don't have to be the flashiest member of the family to shape the hearts and minds of the future generation.

No matter how old a mother is, she watches her middle-aged children for signs of improvement.

—Florida Scott-Maxwell, author and suffragist

Hip

Patricia Shelley Bushman

I always loved my mother and knew she was a special mom. Did I always think she was cool? No, of course not. It often seemed that other mothers were more hip or had more fun with their kids. So it was a big surprise to me to realize, in adulthood, that everyone thought my mom was way cool. When friends speak of my mother, you would think she would be a perfect "Mother of the Year" candidate. And I agree. The glowing terminology is justified. But how did I miss this picture while growing up?

My mom certainly was unlike most mothers in the fifties and sixties. In many ways she was a single parent. My father had a demanding job that took him away on frequent business trips. Then he took a job that was two hours away from home. From the time I was eight, I only saw my dad one night during the week and partially on the weekends. This lasted eight years. My mother was in charge of everything. She had four children with very active lives going in opposite directions. She managed the house and she managed us. Did she complain? Maybe in her prayers at night, but never to us.

Now that I have become a mother I understand why I didn't always think my mom was a barrel of laughs. Why? She was exhausted! She was just plain tired and she never had a break. We kids often laughed at mom because she could never stay awake at the theater or movies. I will never forget the time that she was helping my brother prepare for a test, and she fell asleep right in the middle of asking him a question. Poor Mother! I wish I could go back in time and be more understanding of her situation. I should have washed the dishes without her asking me to. I should have picked up my clothes without her asking me to. I should have surprised her by doing something to help her out. But I didn't. I didn't understand then how difficult a time my mother was having.

As she was serving her own family, she served others within the Church and the community with the few extra hours that she had. After we were grown she had even more time to help friends, extended family, sisters in the gospel, and even strangers. I also saw how my mother was an inspiration to other young moms. Once she was in a ward with several moms whose husbands were professional athletes. Their husbands were on the road frequently, just like my dad. My mom was someone they could turn to for advice and comfort. I realize that my mother's fortitude has been a role model for many other women.

Do my kids think I am special? Do they appreciate me? Only now and then, and it is getting less frequent by the day. Is it frustrating to do so much and have it go unnoticed? Naturally. But I am my mother's daughter. Even if my children do not realize my sacrifices now, the future promises a dawning revelation of my love for them. In one respect, however, I have deviated from my mother's stoicism. When I am exhausted, I tell my children why I am tired and how sometimes I need a rest. My kids still won't think I am hip, but maybe one day they will.

You become about as exciting as your food blender. The kids come in, look you in the eye, and ask if anybody's home.

—Erma Bombeck, humorist

A suburban mother's role is to deliver children obstetrically once, and by car forever after.

—Peter De Vries, American satirist

Your modern teenager is not about to listen to advice from an old person, defined as a person who remembers when there was no Velcro.

—Dave Barry, humorist

Mothers of teenagers know why some animals eat their young.

—Anonymous

Little children, headache; big children, heartache.

—Italian proverb

Grumpy Mama

Heather Sundahl

Just this week at the market I became that woman people look at with embarrassment and disgust, the one in her sweats, yelling at her sticky-faced kids, making threats she'll never live up to—the one I swore I'd never be. It was my fault. I broke my cardinal marketing rule and let the rug rat out of the cart. He wanted to say hi to the lobsters, and then I was too pooped to coax/force him back into the seat. So he hung onto the front of the cart as I s-l -o-w-l -y wheeled him down the aisle.

Of course, he hopped off and I stopped abruptly, growling at him as the lady behind me mashed into my rear end so hard that I am sure there were cart-induced waffle marks on my backside. And she *wouldn't* go around me but loudly huffed and snorted as I was trying to firmly yet calmly get Jonah to stop pushing the cart back into me and my ever-expanding belly. During the next ten minutes this happened three more times on three different aisles with three different grumpy ladies behind me until I finally turned around to the last one and said firmly but not so calmly, "Just go around me, will ya?"

Like dogs and horses who can smell fear on people, Jonah can smell when I've lost my cool, and he goes in for the kill. Two seconds later he staged some fit that my brother Lee would say looks like a recital for the Bratty School of Dance. Instead of whisking him out and leaving as I should have fifteen minutes earlier, I raised my evil right eyebrow and said loud enough for anyone within a two-aisle radius to hear, "Fine, stay here and *live* in the dairy section for all I care!" And I proceeded to head for the cheeses.

Jonah wailed at the top of his lungs, *"No, Mama!* I don't want to live in the dairy section!"

All eyes were on me, the Bad Mom. What did I do? I backpedaled and *lied*.

"Oh, no, sweetie. Mama would never leave you. I was just getting you some of those yummy cheese slices you like . . ."

But everyone there, my kid included, knew my pants were on fire. Fortunately, we both took naps that afternoon. As I was putting him down, he stroked my cheek and, as if to reassure me that I hadn't done any profound damage to his fragile toddler psyche, said, "You're not a grumpy Mama anymore."

Deity aside, no one loves me as unconditionally as my kid. Granted, he pretty much has no choice because I am the source of his food, shelter, clothing, and Hotwheels. But, deserved or not, it is still so satisfying.

When Mama ain't happy, ain't nobody happy.

— Folk saying

I won't lie to you: fatherhood isn't easy like motherhood.

—Homer Simpson

Good News, Bad News

Ardith Walker

As our three children were growing up, I saved the special letters and notes they wrote to me. I got them out the other day, reread them, and realized that mothering is indeed a mixture of good news and bad news. I left the spelling as they wrote it.

Good News
Dear Parents,
I love you very much. Mom you're very pretty. Dad you're a chip off the old block. I like and love you very very much.
Your daughter,
Emily (age nine)

Bad News
Dear Mom,
I am so sorry how I acted in church.
Love,
Emily (age eight)

Good News
Dear Mom,
I love you because you care for me. and you make meals for me. your the best lady I no. you the prettiest lady in the whole world. I love you a lot and I love your smile.
Love,
Scott (age seven)

Bad News
To mom
I'm tired of you bossing me around.
Love,
Scott (age eight)

Good News

Dear Mom,

I want to tell you how much you mean to me. If it weren't for you I'd probably be dead right now. Thank you for all the things you do.

Rebecca (age eight)

Bad News

Dear Mom,

I was folding shopper guides and my leg started to sting and hurt *badley* and so I quit and also Scott was burping and jumping on me so I stopped. I hope you understand. I almost called Linda Crandall [neighbor] because Scott was mean and he poured milk on Emily's Head. My leg hurts so bad I laid it down and it hurts worse than it hurt before so I went to bed and took a Big Drink of milk.

Rebecca (age eight)

Bad News

The good times turn out to be bad times and all of a sudden it gets wers and wers. I mane it. I mane it. I D☹!

Rebecca (age seven after I scolded her)

Now these three children have children of their own. They too are finding that parenting is full of good news and bad news.

It's funny that those things your kids did that got on your nerves seem so cute when your grandchildren do them.

—Anonymous

Am I My Mother's Keeper?

Suzanne Midori Hanna

I know now, more than any other time in my life, that I have become my mother. You wouldn't know it to contrast our lifestyles. It took *me* fifty-three years to recognize the resemblance. Mom was a constant example of baking neighborly pies, befriending neighborhood recluses, praying for her Sunday School class, and pondering out loud what to do about some acquaintance who might have fallen on hard times. I don't bake pies, I hardly know people at church by name, and I work fifty hours a week at a job that doesn't leave me time to search out any recluses except one. Mom.

She's definitely not a recluse by choice, but by condition. At eighty-five, her joints have been ravaged by rheumatoid arthritis, she has Parkinson's disease, and her memory has been reduced to memories of her early life. Now, I am the keeper of Mom's body and Mom's memory. I can tell *her* stories of *her* early life, because she once told them to me. I use *her* dry Irish humor to decide what stories to tell her and to remind her of our longstanding family jokes. I use *her* keen intuition to know what to do for her when she can't speak for herself. I know not to ask, "What can I do?" I just know what to do and I do it, just as she would have years ago.

I know how to brush over those times when she is embarrassed that someone has to help her. I use *her* kind compassion to understand why she can't always be herself, and I use *her* perseverance to wait and enjoy those few times when she is very much still herself. For example, even when she doesn't speak more than a few words a day, I may ask, "Mom, how is your cough?" and she may reply with encouragement, "All's quiet on the western front!"

I keep her comfortable, and I keep her favorite things nearby. With *her* zest for getting things done and making a

118

difference, I keep her caregivers organized and paid. I keep my house organized so she can live here without driving me out. Heaven knows I need all the help I can get!

She has always been so invested in giving life, sustaining life, and enriching life. That is what I saw and what I learned. When my brother lay in a coma, she was fully prepared to take Phillip home in any condition and care for him. As we shared that sacred moment at his bedside when the monitors stopped and the veil opened for him, I vowed that if I had another chance to be with a loved one when heaven meets earth, I would seek the privilege. Those silent moments were the most expansive education I've ever had.

As I keep Mother, only *I* know that the road will eventually turn a corner. I didn't really sign on to be the keeper of her life. When I put her pills down the stomach tube (recommended because she can't swallow pills), I pause at the power of this gesture. It's not the doctor or the nurse. It's me. When she can no longer swallow food, shall I march on, just as Peggy would have always done? Or do she and I let go so that God can be the keeper?

Somehow, all the usual questions—"What would Jesus do?" "What would Mother do?"—don't bring an easy answer. How much should I do? Should I be keeping her alive, or should I be keeping her comfortable? I now see that these are two different things. The one thing I have never seen Mom do is give up. Although she has an advance directive, it only declares that she doesn't want measures that keep her in a persistent vegetative state. Swell. That doesn't help me much now!

However, even though she never gave up on anybody or on life, she also never gave up on the Lord. She lived by the Spirit. She was never so busy serving that she couldn't stop and listen. "Be thou humble and the Lord thy God shall lead thee by the hand and give thee answer to thy prayers." That was her motto.

Sometimes I think about the end, whenever that might be. When we dress her body, it won't be me getting her ready for church or for the doctor. It won't be her favorite pink nightie with tiny blue rosebuds. We won't be anointing her throat with Mentholatum to loosen up congestion. "For now we see through a glass darkly, but then shall we know even as we are known." She was always so proud of the temple dress she made herself. Soft and lacy, it is a statement that the kingdom of God has room for the independently faithful. After all, she comes from a long line of independent pioneer women. So, I am also the keeper of her dress, her robe, and her apron. One of her favorite lines is, "All arrayed in spotless white, we will dwell 'mid truth and light." And so we will dress her in spotless white.

I am my mother's keeper, and she is her daughter's keeper. She keeps me with her close to the veil. She keeps me living in another world. I asked for this privilege. A kind Father in Heaven keeps us both suspended, waiting until the time is right. He keeps her spirit and her time. My burden is lifted. When the time is right, I'll know what to do, and I'll do it. All I have to do is keep pace and be ready. Maybe that's what the wait is really all about. . . .

Tempus Fugit or Why I Don't Do Scrapbooks

Kristine Haglund Harris

Lots of Mormon women make nifty scrapbooks of their kids' and their family's lives. I don't. Sometimes I feel bad about that. I worry that my kids will feel deprived if all the events of their young lives are not recorded in carefully cropped snapshots, with cute die-cut figures and fancy paper borders. For a long time I thought my resistance to scrap booking was just my mild grammar-snobbishness against turning nouns like "scrapbook" into verbs combined with a lack of time. But now I have a few minutes in my days, and I could, if I really wanted to, get around to making those scrapbooks. I still haven't.

Here's why: I don't think they work.

I think people make scrapbooks because they are trying to keep time from slipping through their fingers. Having a child makes you conscious of time in an acute and often painful way. When I was twenty-seven, it was easy for me to think that I was pretty much the same as I had been at twenty-one. But even if I can sometimes think, at thirty-four, that I am pretty much the same as I was when I was twenty-seven (just a "little" fatter and more wrinkled, really!), there is this hulking sixty-pound, seven-year-old next to me, who was just a seven-pound lump of sounds and smells when I was twenty-seven.

I remember when we were leaving the hospital, being sad that he was two whole days old, and it didn't even make sense to give his age in hours anymore. And I shocked myself with a bout of strenuous weeping when he was a month old, and I had to pack away the tiniest T-shirts. At every stage, along with the joy of new discovery, there is the nagging grief of *never again*: look! he's eating cereal (someday soon he'll be weaned); look! he's crawling (someday he will walk away from me); look! he's going to school (he'll learn things I don't teach him); look! he can read (the world is his; he is escaping the home I have so carefully made). And always the aching knowledge that he and I will not be here, in this minute, together again.

A scrapbook is not enough to assuage that grief—it will not bring me back the sweet twenty-pound, six-month-old who made my arms hurt with his delicious chubbiness; it will not smell like the back of his baby neck or his grassy, three-year-old sweat; it will not really hold the awkward one-gigantic-permanent-tooth Cyclops grin that makes it so hard for me to yell at him today. A scrapbook will only be a cruel tease.

There are, of course, many things about motherhood that are impossible to anticipate, but for me the quotidian grief of watching my growing children has been the most shocking. Of course, I knew I would cry when they went to kindergarten, when they graduated from elementary school. I assumed that puberty and teenagerdom would bring *lots* of tears. But I didn't know that so many days would be full of such mixed emotions, that letting out the hem of a dress could feel so profoundly sad, or that I would ever be filled with such rage at the people who draw the arbitrary lines between "Little Kid" and "Big Kid" sizes in the clothing catalogs.

And somehow it feels right. Some days I think I can actually feel my heart stretching to hold all the contradictions, and I think about how Enoch's heart "swelled wide as eternity" when he saw God's love and grief for his children and began to understand what it meant to be a parent.

Mother, I love you. Mother, I do.
Father in Heaven has sent me to you.
When I am near you, I love to hear you
singing so softly that you love me too.
Mother, I love you, I love you, I do.

—"Mother, I Love You," *Sing With Me*, D-16

Who can find a virtuous woman? For her price is far above rubies. . . . She girdeth her loins with strength, and strengtheneth her arms. . . . She stretcheth out her hand to the poor; yea, she reacheth forth her hands to the needy. . . . Strength and honour are her clothing; and she shall rejoice in time to come. She openeth her mouth with wisdom; and in her tongue is the law of kindness. . . . Give her of the fruit of her hands; and let her own works praise her in the gates.

—Proverbs 31:10, 17, 20, 25–26, 31

A convert to The Church of Jesus Christ of Latter-day Saints, Linda Hoffman Kimball lives near Chicago with her husband, Christian. Her three remarkable children think they are all grown up now and are living fascinating lives out of her nest.

Linda, who holds a bachelor's degree from Wellesley College and a master of fine arts degree from Boston University, is a columnist for the on-line interfaith magazine Beliefnet.com and for Exponent II, an LDS women's quarterly newspaper. She is the author of *Chocolate Chips & Charity: Visiting Teaching in the Real World* and *Raspberries & Relevance: Enrichment in the Real World,* published by Cedar Fort. She has also written two humorous novels, *Home to Roost* and *The Marketing of Sister B;* and a picture book for children, *Come With Me on Halloween.*

An artist, poet, photographer, and dog lover, Linda serves as a visiting teacher and Relief Society president in the North Shore First Ward, Wilmette Illinois Stake.

Photo by Thomas Balsamo.

9 26575 78499 5